SAFETY FIRST

A safety and security handbook
for aid workers

Shaun Bickley

Save the Children is the world's leading independent children's rights organisation, with members in 29 countries and operational programmes in more than 100. We fight for children's rights and deliver lasting improvements to children's lives worldwide.

 Save the Children

Published by
Save the Children UK
1 St John's Lane
London EC1M 4AR
UK

First published 2003
Second revised version first published 2010

© International Save the Children Alliance 2010

Registered Charity No. 1076822

ISBN 978 1 84187 127 1

Typeset by Grasshopper Design Company
Printed by Page Bros (Norwich) Ltd

CONTENTS

FOREWORD

The reality is that children in the greatest need of healthcare, food, education and protection are often located in those areas that present the greatest safety and security risks to our staff. The tragic deaths of our aid worker colleagues in recent years highlight the unprecedented levels of hostility and violence to which we are increasingly exposed in the course of our work.

Save the Children's most precious resource is our people, whose safety and security is paramount. Our mandate to provide children in insecure environments with much-needed assistance must be balanced with our responsibility to ensure staff safety and security. Save the Children is committed to maximising our impact on vulnerable children, while minimising safety and security risks to our staff, and ensuring that they receive training, support and information to reduce their risk exposure.

Key to creating a safer working environment is a collective sense of awareness and responsibility. Each member of staff is ultimately responsible for their own safety and security. It is essential that we understand the different risks we face in the field and how to behave in order to reduce these risks to ourselves and our colleagues, which ultimately increases our ability to bring about positive and lasting change for children.

This edition of *Safety First* assembles the best available information on how we can work safely in today's challenging humanitarian environments. It provides practical advice to staff on dealing with safety and security issues as part of delivering our programmes for and with children around the world.

Jasmine Whitbread
Chief Executive
Save the Children

ABOUT THE AUTHOR

Shaun Bickley has extensive field experience managing relief programmes in conflict-prone areas including Afghanistan, Chechnya, Liberia, Pakistan and Sudan. He now works as an independent consultant and trainer to international humanitarian and development organisations, advising on staff security and safety issues, strengthening organisational risk management provision, developing guidance and training materials, and providing training to staff.

ACKNOWLEDGEMENTS

Thanks to Heather Hughes (Oxfam), Jan Davis, Rob Lowe and Stuart Castell (Castell Communication Solutions), Gay Harper, Adrian Uden, Brendan Paddy, Gareth Owen, Lewis Sida, Leonie Lonton, Paul Nolan, Marilyn Thomson, Wendwessen Kitaw, Chris Bowley and Rob Gayton for their feedback and ideas during the writing of the previous edition of *Safety First*.

Thanks also to Ian Trask, Jane Gibreel, Sarah Murphy, Michael O'Neill, Aleksandar Jovkovic, Craig Maartens, Rafael Khusnutdinov, Naomi Bourne, Samantha Wakefield and Ravi Wickremasinghe at Save the Children for their comments and support in updating this latest edition.

I must also mention Kara Brydson, whose support and sharp editorial eye have prevented many mistakes and lapses in concentration.

Two aid workers kidnapped in Haiti

Aid workers shot dead in Pakistan

Spy claims put aid workers in danger

Aid workers evacuated as fighting intensifies

Aid work increasingly dangerous as attacks soar

Aid workers abducted in Darfur

Aid worker seized by Somali gunmen

Four aid workers killed in Afghanistan

Aid workers under fire

Mogadishu, Somalia, 2007

Today, aid agencies experience numerous security challenges, including high levels of violence directed at their staff.

INTRODUCTION

Few issues in recent years have grabbed the attention of the humanitarian aid community more than the increasing problem of insecurity. Around the world, humanitarian workers are being targeted as never before. According to the UN, international aid work has now become one of the world's most hazardous professions.* However, unlike in other hazardous occupations, the risk to aid workers comes mainly in the form of *intentional* violence, as aid workers regularly face being harassed, attacked, kidnapped, or worse.

Although working in challenging environments will always carry a degree of risk, many of the dangers facing agency staff are avoidable or, at the very least, can be substantially reduced. As an aid worker it is essential that you develop an awareness of your own personal security, and understand how your actions or inaction in a particular environment can jeopardise your own safety and that of your colleagues.

NEW THREATS, NEW CHALLENGES FOR AID WORKERS

In recent decades, aid workers have increasingly found themselves operating in complex and rapidly changing socio-political environments. As a result, they face numerous risks in providing vital assistance to communities torn apart by conflict and civil unrest. Providing assistance during armed conflicts has always been dangerous but, until recently, aid

*T Deen, *International Aid Work a Deadly Profession*, Inter Press Service, 2006.

1

workers were rarely the direct targets of violence; agencies, working closely with communities, built acceptance, reputation and trust, which in turn afforded them a degree of security. For a long time it was assumed that as long as you remained independent and neutral, no one would see you as a threat Today, however, there are major challenges to these traditional assumptions. Humanitarian agencies operating in Afghanistan, Pakistan, Somalia and Sudan, for example, now find themselves the targets of attacks, having lost the tacit protection necessary for them to operate safely. Even away from these high-profile contexts, aid agencies experience numerous security challenges, including high levels of violence directed at their national and international staff.

This degree of insecurity clearly influences the level of assistance that aid agencies can provide to beneficiary communities. In some cases, because of security concerns, programmes have had to be curtailed, or organisations have been forced to operate only in areas considered to be relatively safe. In other cases, to ensure a continued presence, aid agencies have had to change their approach by switching to 'remote-control/managed' operations. While this may indeed enable an agency to retain a presence in an area and to continue with its programmes there, the result of this kind of approach can be that the risks are transferred to national colleagues.

While the degree of risk varies from country to country, safety and security incidents can occur in *all* operational areas. Crime is widespread in many of the countries in which aid agencies operate, and it is therefore a significant threat to aid workers. More than 50% of security incidents affecting aid agencies and their staff are associated with crime and banditry.* In environments where resources are scarce, the valuable supplies and equipment that agencies control – such as food stocks, vehicles or communication equipment – undoubtedly make them the target of criminal gangs and looters. Of course, the risks faced by aid workers are not only associated with security-related issues. In many contexts, vehicle accidents, natural disasters and work-related hazards also present a significant risk to staff.

---

* K Van Brabant, *Operational Security Management in Violent Environments*, Good Practice Review 8, ODI, London, 2000.

Good safety and security management must be an integral part of all programmes, not just those affected by conflict or political violence.

STAFF SECURITY, SAFETY AND HEALTH

The nature of today's operational environment is clearly changing. Organisations now have to balance the considerable pressures involved in achieving and maintaining access within insecure environments, and their responsibility to ensure the safety and security of staff. If an organisation is to fulfil its responsibility to ensure a safe and secure working environment for its staff, it must establish a comprehensive approach across the organisation to manage *all* the risks to which staff are exposed in the course of their work.

Safeguarding staff should be the fundamental concern of your organisation. It is important that you and your colleagues do not focus purely on security risks to the detriment of staff health and safety risks. Despite the increase in security risks, the vast majority of aid workers working in the field still face significant risks of ill health through injury, illness or stress. Vehicle and work-related accidents, malaria, and cumulative stress can affect you whether you're working in a secure or an insecure environment. Therefore, good safety and security management must be considered an integral part of *all* programmes in all countries, not just those affected by conflict or political violence.

WHY *SAFETY FIRST?*

No book can possibly provide all the answers on how to respond when faced with insecurity, or what to do to reduce the risks to your health and safety while working in the field. You will always be required to make judgements based on your awareness of the situation and the nature of the threat you're faced with. Security awareness isn't difficult and it doesn't require any specialist knowledge. We all have some level of security awareness; *Safety First's* primary aim is to enhance and develop this awareness by introducing aid workers to the basic principles of security management and by providing them with practical guidance on dealing with a range of safety and security issues.

Much of what is written here is basic common sense. *Safety First* provides useful reminders and easy-reference chapters to be consulted as safety and security issues arise. Not only is this book essential reading for staff about to take up their first field positions, it should be kept to hand as an indispensable reference for even the most seasoned aid worker. *Safety First* is one tool in a wider toolkit of material that is available in the humanitarian sector for managing and reducing safety and security risks.

Safety First, originally issued in 1995, was substantially rewritten in 2003 to reflect significant developments in the non-governmental organisation (NGO) approach to dealing with insecurity, and to reflect a greater understanding of the various risks facing aid workers. Now, *Safety First* has been updated to reflect emerging safety and security challenges and to ensure that it continues to provide practical and relevant guidance to staff in minimising safety and security risks associated with their work.

WHO IS *SAFETY FIRST* FOR?

Safety First has been developed primarily as a field guide for both nationally and internationally recruited staff working in Save the Children offices and field sites throughout the world. However, the issues it covers are just as relevant to staff working with other agencies, and therefore it can offer important guidance to all aid workers in the field or individuals considering working in the humanitarian sector.

Safety First is aimed at all levels of staff, from the most experienced senior managers to the newest members of the team. A few of the issues discussed may seem to be more relevant for managers or those with direct responsibility for staff safety and security This is a dangerous assumption: all staff have a responsibility for their own safety and security, and that of their colleagues.

It's vital that field staff of all levels and job descriptions understand the basic principles of managing safety and security. In order to minimise safety and security risks, everyone has to work as part of a team in which each individual understands why certain actions are necessary and will put these into practice effectively and without delay.

1 BASIC PRINCIPLES OF MANAGING SECURITY

Aid work can be dangerous and unpredictable. However, good safety and security management can enable an agency to deliver effective programmes while minimising risks to staff, assets, and the organisation. How your agency manages these risks depends on where you're working, the nature of your programmes, and the types of risks that exist. Organisations differ from each other in their character, and their ways of dealing with safety and security issues will vary accordingly The various mandates and principles that shape your agency's programmes will also dictate which risks it is willing to accept and the approaches it will adopt to minimise these risks. Despite these differences in approach, there are basic principles of managing safety and security that all agencies adhere to.

Creating a safe and secure working environment requires careful planning, commitment, and a collective sense of awareness and responsibility. Managing safety and security is fundamentally about good programme management The types of programmes your agency undertakes and how these are implemented will affect, and be affected by, the risks to which you and your colleagues are exposed. For safety and security management to be truly effective it must be fully integrated into programme design and management, and not be seen as a separate issue.

Effective safety and security management requires a systematic process that maximises the safety and security of staff while affording them the greatest possible freedom to carry out their work.

Save the Children's policy

Save the Children is committed to minimising safety and security risks to staff and ensuring staff are given training, support and information to reduce their risk exposure while maximising the impact for children.

Save the Children Safety and Security Policy and Standards, February 2010.

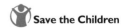 **Save the Children**

SECURITY MANAGEMENT FRAMEWORK

Effective safety and security management requires a systematic process for analysing the operating environment, identifying risks, and adopting appropriate measures and procedures that maximise the safety and security of staff while affording them the greatest possible freedom to carry out their work.

The security management framework opposite demonstrates how the safety and security management process can be divided into individual components:

- **Assessment** The first stage in the security management framework is to develop a thorough understanding of the operational environment. Aid agencies often operate in politically and socially complex environments that change rapidly. In order to adapt security management accordingly, and anticipate possible risks to staff, field teams must understand and critically analyse the environment around them. If you analyse the operational context in sufficient detail, you'll be able to draw out the information needed to make a realistic assessment of the risks. A comprehensive risk assessment should determine both the likelihood and the potential impact of the various threats that staff face.

- **Planning**. You then need to identify different mitigation strategies that can be implemented to reduce these risks The strategies you adopt will depend on the risk assessment, your organisation's values and mandate, and its programme activities in that particular context. You should then put these strategies into practice through the development of safety and security plans. Safety and security plans must be established for the country and, where relevant, for particular programme areas, and should include standard operating procedures (SOPs) and contingency measures or plans for foreseeable high-risk incidents.

- **Implementation**. Ensuring the effective day-to-day management of safety and security issues, and compliance by all staff, is often the most challenging aspect of the process. Operational safety and security management – concerning the routine actions, measures and procedures that govern how staff work in the office, travel to the field,

Security management framework

ASSESS

Operational context analysis
- General situation
- Conflict and political violence
- Criminal activity

Risk assessment
- Threat identification and analysis
- Vulnerability assessment
- Risk analysis

PLAN

Security strategies

Acceptance

Protection   Deterrence

Safety and security plans
- Standard operating procedures (SOPs)
- Contingency plans
- Security levels and indicators
- Roles and responsibilities

IMPLEMENT

Operational safety and security management
- Staff induction and briefings
- Site safety and security
- Travel and movements
- Vehicle safety
- Communications
- Information management
- Incident management

MONITOR

Incident monitoring
- Incident reporting
- Incident analysis and mapping

REVIEW

Security reviews
- Safety and security plan update
- Minimum standards audit
- Safety and security management review
- Post-incident investigation

Influences

Internal factors
- Agency values and mandate
- Programme activities
- Global safety and security policy
- Other organisational policies and procedures
- Crisis management plan
- Staff competencies
- Security training
- Resources

External factors
- Government and local authorities
- Geography and climate
- Infrastructure
- Society and culture
- Inter-agency collaboration
- Media
- Image and perception of NGOs

Source: Adapted from K Van Brabant, *Operational Security Management in Violent Environments*, Good Practice Review 8, ODI, London, 2000.

or relax after work – is often perceived as overly restrictive. However, when staff fully understand the risks, they're more likely to accept the actions necessary to mitigate them. Once safety and security management is embedded into everyday programme management, staff will see that it enables them to have greater access to the communities they are working with and to work more effectively in insecure environments.

- **Monitoring** Thorough safety and security management requires ongoing monitoring, analysis and mapping of all security incidents. If you make sure that this is done for each security incident that occurs in a particular context, you'll acquire new information and a better understanding of the overall security situation. As your awareness improves, you must continually review each component of the security management framework to ensure that it remains appropriate to the changing situation.

- **Review**. Security management is a dynamic process and must be continually reviewed. Safety and security plans should be updated and circulated to staff as a matter of routine to ensure plans remain relevant and effective. It is also important to carry out periodic reviews of safety and security management in each country to determine whether it meets your organisation's minimum standards, and to ensure that the most effective management practice is in place. In the event of a serious incident involving staff, there should be a detailed investigation into the various decisions and actions taken and, subsequently, a review of the safety and security measures in place The analysis and recommendations raised in these various reviews should feed back into the relevant components of the security management framework.

A number of additional factors will influence the management of safety and security at each stage in the security management framework. These include:

- **Internal factors**. An organisation's ability to manage safety and security in the field will be shaped by many internal factors, such as the agency's mandate and values, its programme activities, the various policies and procedures in place, the level of training provided to staff, and the material and financial resources available.

- **External factors**. Agencies do not operate in a vacuum and many external factors will affect their ability to manage insecurity. For example, in highly politicised environments the sensitive relationships that often exist between aid agencies and authorities (government, police, military or rebel factions, etc) may restrict the security measures that can be utilised. Equally, the actions, or inaction, of other agencies in the same environment will affect how an agency manages its own security.

UNDERSTANDING THE CONTEXT

As an aid worker, you need to be constantly inquisitive about the environment in which you are working This includes seeking information about the country or region and its historical, political, economic and social situation and the culture of its people. You must also consider how you, your programme, your agency, and agencies in general might be perceived in that environment. You won't reach this level of understanding overnight, but you'll be able to develop it through continual analysis and monitoring, using existing information (eg, reports produced by other agencies and political analysts) and your own research.

To understand the wider operational context you need to become aware of, for example, the significant moments and actors in the country's history; key actors and groups, and their agendas in the current political situation; and key national and local economic interests and their impact on the levels of poverty and crime. As your analysis advances you gradually develop a profile of the country that will help you begin to understand the various risks and threats that exist.

If you develop positive relationships and interact appropriately within the community, this will have a significant impact on your security. In order to understand the various social and cultural dynamics, it's important to develop an awareness of cultural norms, practices and customs: how people behave and why; how they dress; what is acceptable behaviour for men and women in different cultural contexts; how they view you and the work you are doing; how decisions are made in the community; and how power and status are accorded (by age, gender, wealth, ethnicity or religion).

11

In areas affected by conflict or political violence it's important to acquire a deeper understanding of what is happening and why This more detailed analysis will enable you to anticipate any changes that might affect security. In order to understand the dynamics of the conflict or violence, the position your agency occupies, and the resulting threats and risks, you must develop a greater awareness of the following:

- **Parties involved**. Identify who the different actors/groups are and what they are fighting for. Examine their relationships with other groups and try to determine how these different groups are organised and what level of control they have.
- **Causes**. Investigate what appears to be the main causes of the conflict or violence, and consider how these may have changed over time.
- **Areas affected**. Identify the areas in which the fighting or violence occurs, or has taken place in the past. Consider which areas are strategically more important and why.
- **Relationships with civilian population**. Determine whether certain groups have a strong support base in the community, or whether they have a more abusive relationship with the civilian population. Consider how your programme or presence could threaten and/or undermine these relationships.
- **Nature of violence**. Examine whether terror tactics are adopted by any particular group and whether violence is orchestrated or spontaneous. Identify who their main targets are and why.
- **Political or military developments**. Consider what impact political or military developments at the national, regional or global levels will have on the conflict or level of violence in the area where you are operating.

In areas with significant criminal activity it's important to determine in more detail the level and types of crime that exist in different locations, and therefore how likely it is that you will become a target and why. In areas of conflict, often conflict and crime are intrinsically linked. For example, some groups in the conflict may rely on criminal activity, such as kidnapping or looting, as their source of funds. Therefore, an understanding of this link should form part of your wider analysis of the conflict. To assess the risks associated with crime, you need to investigate in more detail the following:

- **Types of crime.** Research the different types of crime that occur in your area and who appears to be responsible for these crimes.
- **Where it occurs.** Identify any patterns with regard to the location of incidents, to determine whether certain areas are more at risk than others.
- **Who is targeted.** Examine whether crime is widespread or whether particular groups, including humanitarian agencies, are being targeted.
- **Nature of criminal activity.** Consider whether criminal activity is organised or opportunistic. Determine whether weapons and violence are associated with these crimes.

It's important to gather information from numerous and varied sources in order to acquire a balanced and realistic impression of a situation. In some locations gathering information is very sensitive and can put you and your colleagues at risk, so you must make sure you are adequately briefed on the risks involved.

ASSESSING THE RISKS

Everyone faces risk in their daily lives. You will try, often subconsciously, to reduce a risk by adopting a measure to make yourself less vulnerable to it: for example, choosing to use a pedestrian crossing rather than crossing a road at its busiest point. This kind of ad hoc assessment is not adequate in the humanitarian environment, however, given the scale and nature of the risks, many of which you may be able to identify in advance.

A structured risk assessment process will help you and your colleagues to identify the likely threats in your location and to determine the degree to which you are vulnerable to those threats. With this better understanding of the risks you'll be able to make more informed decisions about taking effective measures to deal with them.

Assessing risks must not be a one-off event. A continuous re-evaluation of possible risks will ensure that you have appropriate security measures in place at all times.

Developing and maintaining a constant awareness and understanding of your surroundings is the first step in assessing risk.

Identifying the threats

Developing and maintaining a constant awareness and understanding of threats that exist in your surroundings is the first step in assessing risk.

A threat is any danger that may result in harm or injury to staff, or loss of or damage to your agency's property or programme.[*] Given the range of potential threats, and that each one may require a different approach, it's important to identify and analyse all of them. Talking to colleagues, other

---

[*] J T Dworken, *Threat Assessment: Training Module for NGOs Operating in Conflict Zones and High Crime Areas*, OFDA/InterAction, 1998.

agencies, and authorities and individuals in the community will help you determine where, when and why threats occur, their outcomes, who the victims and perpetrators are, and any patterns that emerge.

Threats can generally be divided into two groups: those that are part and parcel of your working environment and could affect anybody in any location (inherent threats), and threats that particularly target your organisation, an individual staff member, or humanitarian agencies in general (targeted threats).

Types of threats

Inherent threats (Non-targeted threats)	Targeted threats
• **Work and travel** – ill health; work place accidents; vehicle accidents; air crashes; boat accidents, etc. • **Natural hazards** – earthquakes; floods; avalanches; wildlife, etc. • **Wrong place, wrong time** – demonstrations and rallies; indiscriminate violence; looting; crossfire; military actions, etc. • **Indiscriminate weapons** – mines and unexploded ordnance (UXOs); shelling and aerial bombardment; chemical and biological weapons, etc.	• **Crime** – armed robbery or theft; arson; ambush; carjacking; bribery, extortion and fraud, etc. • **Acts of violence** – bodily harm; assault; sexual violence, etc. • **Acts of terror** – bombs/improvised explosive devices (IEDs); suicide attacks; shootings/assassinations, etc. • **Staff disappearance** – detention; arrest; abduction; kidnapping, etc. • **Psychological intimidation** – harassment; death threats, etc.

In general, inherent threats are more predictable, and provided that you and your colleagues use common sense and adhere to basic safety and security procedures, it should be possible to reduce the risks. Targeted threats are far more difficult to respond to, often requiring you to develop a heightened level of awareness and to adopt more stringent security measures and procedures.

Considering your vulnerability

It's important to understand why individual staff members, your agency, or humanitarian agencies in general are more or less likely than others to be affected by the threats in the same environment.

How vulnerable you, your agency and its assets are to different threats can be directly or indirectly influenced by a number of factors. For example, you may be more at risk than other organisations because of the location of your programme sites (accommodation, offices, warehouses, etc), or because of the population or groups you work with. You may be more at risk because your programmes are perceived as aiding one particular group, or undermining another. You may be more vulnerable to a particular threat because of your gender, ethnicity, nationality or perceived wealth, or even because of the position you hold or the responsibilities associated with your job. Your vulnerability may be affected by the lack of, or inappropriateness of, your security measures or perhaps because staff fail to comply with security procedures.

Determining the risks

Balancing the operational demands of responding to a particular situation or working in a particular area against the need to reduce exposure to security risks is a constant juggling act. It is neither possible nor effective to put in place extensive security measures to deal with every possible threat. You must analyse the different threats to determine which pose the greatest risk. These should then become the focus of your security measures.

To calculate the degree of risk, assess each threat in two ways: first, ask yourself what is the likelihood of the threat materialising; secondly, ask what will be its impact if it does. The degree of risk is highest in the case of an incident that is most likely to occur and that will have the greatest impact on an individual, programme or organisation.

For example, your analysis, as reflected in the risk analysis table opposite, may indicate that an incident of petty theft is very likely, but its impact on the organisation would be negligible. Alternatively, although the impact of

Risk analysis table

		IMPACT				
		Negligible	**Minor**	**Moderate**	**Severe**	**Critical**
LIKELIHOOD	**Very likely**	Petty theft				
	Likely			Harassment by security forces		
	Moderately likely			Armed robbery	Major road traffic accident	
	Unlikely					
	Very unlikely					Kidnapping

Very high risk	Immediate response and extreme measures required. Is the risk acceptable?
High risk	Implement specific safety and security measures and contingency plans
Medium risk	Significant safety and security measures required
Low risk	Requires heightened awareness and additional procedures
Very low risk	Managed by routine security and safety procedures

Source: Adapted from *Security Risk Management: NGO Approach*, InterAction, 2009

a member of staff being kidnapped would be critical for the individual and the organisation, your analysis may demonstrate that it's very unlikely to happen to you or your colleagues. In both these cases, it's important to recognise that despite being low-risk, these threats nevertheless exist, and additional measures must be in place to deal with them. However, you shouldn't focus all your attention on dealing with these to the detriment of other, higher-risk threats, such as harassment by security forces, armed robbery and vehicle accidents. You need to understand all the threats in detail, so that you can identify which must be addressed, make informed decisions about which security measures to adopt, and avoid adopting unnecessary measures.

What is an acceptable risk?

Not all agencies will accept the same level of risk; a particular agency may interpret a security situation differently or, because of its mandate, will be more or less willing than others to accept higher levels of risk. Some agencies may decide to remain in a high-risk area because they feel that the benefits to the local population outweigh the risks to which their staff are exposed. Others, however, may be unwilling to operate in the same environment.

Each agency, and individual staff member, must consider what level of risk they are willing to accept. Ideally, the level of risk that you regard as acceptable for yourself will be compatible with your organisation's position. If not, you should discuss with your organisation whether you should remain in that location. If you are unhappy with the risks, you always have the right to leave.

SECURITY PLANNING AND DOCUMENTATION

Having gained an understanding of the risks associated with your location, the next step is to identify ways to minimise them. Often an agency's approach to minimising risks to staff concentrates on the development of local or 'field-based' safety and security documents. Although these are of course important in themselves, what's crucial is the strategic thinking behind them. To be truly effective, the safety and security measures and procedures you adopt must be part of a well-considered strategic approach to security that suits your context and organisation.

Security strategies

The different approaches used to manage security risks fall into three broad strategies: acceptance, protection and deterrence.* The acceptance-based strategy seeks to reduce or remove threats by developing and maintaining widespread acceptance, among all actors, of your presence and work. The protection-based strategy focuses on reducing your vulnerability or exposure to certain risks through the implementation of procedures or using equipment to secure yourself against these risks. The principal aim of the deterrence-based strategy is to attempt to reduce or remove threats by posing a counter-threat that will deter or influence aggressors.

Acceptance strategy

How you and your agency are perceived has a fundamental effect on your security. It's a mistake to assume that everyone will understand the concept of humanitarian aid. Similarly, don't assume that various groups in the community know who your organisation is, what work you are doing and why. All staff must be fully aware of the programme's objectives and be able to communicate them to the different actors your agency interacts with. If the local community and power structures have a greater understanding of the aims of your programme, this can bring about wider acceptance of, and support for, your presence and activities, and ultimately this can enhance your security. For example, acceptance by a community could deter those criminal elements over which they have some influence from acting against you. However, if the community is unaware of, or has negative feelings towards, your agency or its programme, criminal groups may feel they can act against you with impunity. Key elements of an acceptance strategy include:

- **Relationships**. It's important to develop and maintain good relationships with individuals, community leaders, governments and authorities – even local commanders. These can increase understanding and appreciation of your work, which may in turn lead to a concern

---

* K Van Brabant, *Operational Security Management in Violent Environments*, Good Practice Review 8, ODI, London, 2000.

for your safety. At the same time, you need to maintain a transparent balance in your relationships, although you may have to distance yourself from some because of how they may be perceived by others. For example, socialising with government officials may be viewed with suspicion by opposition groups.

- **Negotiation**. In highly politicised environments it's important to obtain from all the different actors their consent for your organisation to operate freely and unhindered, and have access to the areas of humanitarian need. For example, even if you may have permission from the relevant authorities to operate in certain areas, other groups may view your presence or activities with suspicion. This lack of acceptance by certain actors could be a major source of threat to you and your colleagues. In some contexts, obtaining the consent of local leaders or armed opposition groups can be very difficult, often requiring lengthy and sensitive negotiations.

- **Participation**. The way in which you identify, design and implement your programmes will either enhance or diminish your acceptance. If the community feel they have a stake in the programme and have been consulted in its design and implementation, this can improve your overall security. For example, a community that is fully supportive and engaged in your programme activities may be able to use their influence to deter criminal groups in the community from acting against you.

- **Dissemination**. Consider how you communicate and what you say about your agency's goals and activities in the media, public meetings, at checkpoints or in the local bar, and what impact this might have on your acceptance. Ensure that these messages are consistent, transparent and broadly communicated to all. For example, as drivers often interact with many different people in the community, it's important that they are aware of, and can communicate positively, the agency's mandate and programme activities.

- **Image and perception**. As well as the explicit messages you communicate, it's equally important to be aware of the implicit messages you may convey through your appearance or behaviour, or what you say and do. Your agency and its staff will convey a variety of images that in some situations may lead to misunderstandings and have a negative effect on your security. For example, excessive displays of wealth through choice of residences and offices, or of agency vehicles, may create resentment among communities and attract attention from criminal groups. Inappropriate behaviour by staff – for example, public drunkenness or unacceptable sexual relations – could aggravate existing tensions in terms of how staff and your agency are perceived. These tensions can provide an ideal focus for those within the community who are seeking to create problems for your agency.

Protection strategy

In the past, many agencies' response to insecurity was to concentrate mainly on protection strategies. These focus on your vulnerability, by removing or limiting your exposure to the various threats. A protection-based approach is of course essential, but it should be supplemented by

Wider acceptance of, and support for, your presence and activities can enhance your security.

other types of approach, since it focuses primarily on dealing with the *threat itself*, rather than on the *cause* of the threat. Key elements of a protection strategy include:

- **Operational policies and procedures**. These are the different organisational mechanisms that aim to enhance security, such as global security policies; safety and security plans; vehicle policies; travel and movement procedures; and curfews and no-go zones. These may also include wider organisational policies and procedures, which may affect or be affected by the security situation.
- **Staff awareness and development**. These measures are aimed at improving staff awareness and include formal staff security briefings and orientations; personal safety and security training; and security management training.
- **Protection devices**. These are the various materials and equipment needed to provide adequate security, such as communications equipment; reliable vehicles; perimeter walls and alarm systems; bomb shelters and sandbagging of windows; and emergency food and water supplies.
- **Security collaboration**. These are security initiatives that agencies are able to carry out together, creating a 'strength in numbers' approach, such as inter-agency security forums; emergency communications tree; joint evacuation plans; and sharing security information and incident reports.

Deterrence strategy

The principle of a deterrence strategy is to try to prevent a threatened incident from occurring by posing a counter-threat to the perpetrators. This security strategy is often the most controversial as there are significant limits to what humanitarian agencies can do to pose a credible counter-threat. Key elements of deterrence strategy include:

- **Suspension and/or withdrawal of activities**. Deterrence may involve the threat of suspension and/or withdrawal of programme activities. For example, if you tell the authorities or local community that unless the security situation improves you will have no option but to suspend your activities, this may encourage them to use their influence over the perpetrators. However, it is difficult to adopt this strategy, because the authorities' or community's influence may be limited, and withdrawal could have a major impact on beneficiaries. Threatening to suspend or withdraw your activities may even result in an increase in security threats – for example, if the perpetrators' main aim is to force you to leave. Most NGOs are neither large nor influential enough on their own for this approach to be effective, so there may need to be a joint approach with other agencies.

- **Diplomatic deterrence**. This involves lobbying or advocating to international actors, such as the UN and governments, to exert pressure on behalf of agencies. For example, an external government may use its influence over, or threaten sanctions against, local powers who either pose a security threat themselves or fail to promote the agencies' security interests.
- **Armed protection**. Although unarmed guards are commonly used at agency facilities around the world, the use of armed guards or escorts is a controversial issue and rarely undertaken by humanitarian agencies, except in extreme circumstances. For example, because of the high risk of kidnapping and hostage-taking in Afghanistan, Somalia, Iraq and Chechnya, some agencies use armed guards to protect their staff.
- **Military deterrence**. This is the least common form of deterrence strategy and a difficult issue for many agencies because of inconsistencies with their mandates or concerns regarding the increasing militarisation of humanitarian action. Military deterrence entails humanitarian agencies receiving direct protection from military forces in an attempt to ensure greater security and safer access. An example is when humanitarian agencies travel in convoys that are protected by international peacekeeping forces.

Balanced approach

The choice of strategy will depend on the level of insecurity and the specific nature of the risks you are trying to mitigate. However, the reality is that no single strategy will address all the security threats that exist. The more effective approach is often one that balances elements of all three security strategies, although more emphasis may be placed on certain aspects as the level of insecurity evolves.

Security strategies

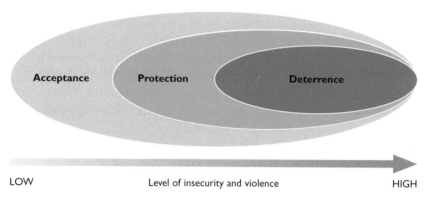

Acceptance Protection Deterrence

LOW Level of insecurity and violence HIGH

Devised by C Williams and S Bickley

For example, in situations where community leaders have some control or influence over certain criminal groups, an acceptance-based strategy may help to strengthen your support within the community, which may also dissuade these criminal groups from targeting you. However, you can't simply rely on the goodwill and support of the community; the risks associated with crime will still remain, so you will also need to carry out additional protection measures and procedures to reduce these risks.

Even in more extreme security risk environments, where the communities and local leaders have no influence over armed groups who are attacking or kidnapping aid workers, and where there is greater emphasis on deterrence-based approaches, it is vital that acceptance-based strategies still form a fundamental part of your security management approach. This will not only help to mitigate other threats existing in that environment, it could enable your agency to resolve a kidnapping incident if this were to happen to you or your colleagues.

Safety and security plans

Safety and security plans, or guidelines, are country-level documents outlining the safety and security measures and procedures, and the resources and information required to implement them. These plans are developed to help you prevent or mitigate security or safety incidents in a manner appropriate for your agency in your particular context.

Developing local safety and security plans – such as drawing up travel and movement procedures, planning for contingencies, agreeing security levels or phases (see 'Security levels and indicators', below), and clarifying roles and responsibilities – must be a team process. This will ensure that all staff understand the issues and make them more likely to 'buy into' and adhere to the measures and procedures in place.

Safety and security plans must be applicable in practical terms. They must be accessible to staff, and should be translated into local languages where necessary. It is vital that these plans are continually reviewed to reflect any changes in the security situation.

Standard operating procedures

Safety and security plans should clearly outline the various standard operating procedures (SOPs). SOPs are designed to ensure that safety and security best practice is maintained on a day-to-day basis and should set out clear parameters for staff (basically the 'dos and don'ts') which, if followed, will help staff to prevent or minimise safety and security risks in that particular location. SOPs can cover a wide variety of issues, such as: personal security; local laws and customs; site security and safety; staff travel and movements; vehicle safety; communications; staff health and welfare; financial management; reporting incidents; and managing information.

Contingency plans

Standard operating procedures are designed to help prevent safety and security incidents happening in the first place. Unfortunately, even with these procedures in place, there is no guarantee that incidents will not occur. In the event of an incident, staff must be prepared to react appropriately to minimise the effects.

Safety and security management plans

All Save the Children Country Offices must develop and maintain a **Country Safety and Security Management Plan (SSMP)**[*] containing information and procedures relating to the security of staff and assets in that particular context. In countries with programme activities in areas for which there are different or additional risks to staff, further location-specific Safety and Security Management Plans may also be needed.

The Country Director is responsible for developing and maintaining the SSMP in conjunction with his/her Safety and Security Focal Point (SSFP), and for ensuring that these plans comply with Save the Children Safety and Security Policy and Standards:

- All SSMPs must be updated at least annually or following significant changes in the operating environment or as a result of a major incident.
- New country programmes must develop and disseminate an SSMP within one month of the initial start-up of the country programme.
- During a Save the Children emergency response, *or after country management decision to respond*, the SSMP must be reviewed and updated (or a new SSMP developed for new programming areas) in

[*] Save the Children Security Policy and Standards – Standard 2, February 2010.

Contingency plans are a set of pre-established procedures and guidelines for staff to follow in order to coordinate a response to an incident. You should develop contingency plans for those risks that are most likely to happen and have the greatest potential impact. You also need them for situations where any response would require significant preparation and information, or would have to be carried out quickly and in a coordinated

light of the changes brought about by the emergency. The revised SSMP must be produced within seven days of the initial emergency declaration and should be taken into account when designing programmes and during their implementation.

- All SSMPs should include an assessment of the threat environment, outlining Save the Children's particular vulnerabilities and the risks to staff; the safety and security policies and procedures; and the roles and responsibilities of staff.

- The SSMP should include contingency plans and standard operating procedures that address: medical evacuation, non-medical evacuation and relocation, suspension of operations, motor vehicle accidents, detention of staff, death of staff, and similar events as determined by the safety and security assessment.

- All staff must be made aware of the contents and authority of the plan; where necessary, local language translation and training should be provided to ensure full understanding of responsibilities.

Detailed guidance on developing SSMPs can be found in the tools that accompany the Save the Children Safety and Security Policy and Standards.

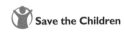 **Save the Children**

manner. Examples include: where there's a serious risk of having to evacuate or relocate staff; medical emergencies; natural disasters; and staff abduction, kidnapping or hostage-taking.

When agencies and their staff are faced with a threatening situation, the way they react is inevitably determined by a judgement made at the time. However, staff will react to it much more effectively if they are well

Every aid worker has a responsibility not only for their own personal security and safety, but for the safety and security of their colleagues.

prepared for it. If you discuss likely scenarios as a team and agree on responses, this will help to ensure that contingency plans will be practical and effective in your context. Even if plans are not implemented exactly as envisioned, contingency planning itself – the process of developing the guidelines – helps staff to respond more rapidly and effectively than if no planning had taken place.

Security levels and indicators

Many agencies employ a system of security levels or phases to indicate different degrees of risk. These systems may be numerical (eg, one to five), colour-coded (eg, green, yellow, red and black) or both. Each number or colour represents the level of risk faced by staff. As the changing security situation progresses through different levels, staff will be required to carry out various prescribed actions, and certain restrictions will be placed on them. All staff must be made aware of the current level or phase in which they are operating. Your team must decide which events in your local environment will indicate a change in the security situation, and therefore require you to step up or step down a level. You must make all staff and your organisation's headquarters aware of any change in security levels as soon as possible.

Although the use of security levels or phases is useful, particularly in comparing one location or country with another, the system has its limits. Security levels can never accurately reflect the important small and subtle changes that may take place and which require you to become more alert. Also, the system implies that there will always be a gradual deterioration in security; in reality, the security situation can very quickly jump from level one to level five.

Security levels

Save the Children operates a system of five security levels to categorise the security situation in a given country or location, according to the level of risk to staff.

These levels are standard across the organisation and must be included in the Country Safety and Security Management Plan.

The following indicators and responses associated with each level do not represent an exhaustive list and are provided as a guide. It is the responsibility of the country Senior Management Team (SMT) to identify specific indicators that signify a change in the security level in their country and to detail additional security measures and procedures that must be implemented in respect of changes in the security level.

Decisions regarding Security Level 1 to 3 can be made at country level. However, decisions regarding Security Level 4 and above must be made in consultation with the respective Regional/Area Director and the Director of Global Programmes and, where possible, the Global Safety and Security Department.

Save the Children

Level	General indicators
Level 1 (Normal)	• Secure situation within the country/area. • No outward signs of significant social disruption or instability. • Crime is within normal limits and a functioning system of justice is in place. • Free and unrestricted movement of staff at all times. • No observable threat to Save the Children staff. • Programme activities continuing as normal.
Level 2 (Tense)	• Significant political, economic and social unrest is present. • High crime, ineffective police and/or justice systems. • Local animosity/hostility towards UN and NGOs, but not directed at Save the Children staff. • Some restrictions on movement of staff in certain locations. • Programme activities carrying on as normal but with a need for extra care and diligence.
Level 3 (Insecure)	• Substantial deterioration in the security situation. • General lawlessness, incidents of rioting or looting reported. • Emergency or martial law declared. • Organised anti-government or terrorist groups threatening government stability. • Assassinations of prominent leaders/politicians. • Terrorist activities or other violence indicates foreigners are being targeted. • Localised incidents of fighting between specific groups, or as a result of military activity. • Staff movement and presence in particular areas, or at particular times, is restricted. • Programme activities restricted.
Level 4 (Dangerous)	• Widespread civil unrest and indiscriminate violence. • Fighting or military actions close to area of operations. • Credible threat against NGOs or towards Save the Children staff. • Staff relocated from particular areas, and possible further relocation of staff. • All staff movements restricted. • Programme activities restricted to essential 'life saving' activities or suspended.
Level 5 (Untenable)	• Fighting or military actions in the immediate vicinity of Save the Children's offices and residences. • Security deteriorated to such an extent that it is considered unsafe, or impossible, to relocate/evacuate from the area/country. • Staff waiting for an opportunity to relocate/evacuate. • No movement of staff at any time unless as part of a relocation/evacuation. • Programme activities suspended.

Security management response	Individual actions
• Develop and maintain strong relations with individuals, community leaders, authorities and local government. • Maintain liaison with other agencies and UN. • Ensure a full security and safety briefing is provided to all staff and visitors, upon arrival, or as part of their local recruitment. • Apply standard operating procedures for staff travel and movement, communications, facility access, etc. • Maintain emergency personnel files for all staff.	• Each individual staff member is responsible for their own security, safety and health. • All staff should proactively monitor the security situation and report any incidents or concerns to their line manager. • All staff must carry Save the Children photo ID card, where appropriate, and emergency contact information.
• As Level 1 • Notify to all staff of increased security level. • Establish regular staff security meetings. • Ensure all staff movements are monitored, and all field travel is limited to daylight hours. • Review and reinforce security measures and procedures. • Establish guards at Save the Children offices and residences. • Establish and test emergency communications tree.	• As Level 1 • All staff should avoid travelling alone, especially at night. • All staff should routinely communicate their movement plans, or any changes, to colleagues.
• As Level 2 • Inform RO and HO of increased security level. • Ensure staff are briefed on security developments and incidents on a routine basis (weekly). • Ensure all staff movements are strictly monitored, including time of departure, estimated time of arrival and persons travelling. • Ensure all travel to field is authorised by the Country Director. • Maintain emergency communications and coordinate with other agencies. Test emergency communications tree weekly. • Review and update evacuation/relocation plans and prepare for possible closure of offices and activities. • Prepare provisions for possible hibernation and store in designated hibernation location. • Ensure regular backup of computer files and store in a secure location.	• As Level 2 • All staff should maintain regular contact with base. • All staff should clearly understand the evacuation/relocation plans and procedures, and prepare an essential grab bag. • All staff should ensure that Save the Children residencies have adequate supplies (water, food, first aid kit, etc) and working emergency communication equipment.
• As Level 3 • Consult with RO and HO regarding suspension of activities and possible relocation/evacuation of staff. • Ensure staff are updated on security situation (daily). • Relocate/evacuate non-essential staff (and dependants) and prohibit visitors. • Nominate and prepare national management team. • Back up data, and identify sensitive documents and data that must be removed or destroyed.	• As Level 3 • All staff should return to base/safe area and await further instruction. • All travel and movements must be authorised by CD. • All staff should have a pre-packed bag of essential items ready and with them at all times.
• As Level 4 • Suspend all programme activities and close office. • Initiate relocation/evacuation plan. • All international staff restricted to designated safe areas and be prepared for immediate evacuation. • National staff relocated to place of origin/safe haven. • Secure assets and remove or destroy sensitive documents and data. • Maintain constant contact with RO and HO, diplomatic mission(s), UN and other agencies until evacuation/relocation can be implemented. • HIBERNATE if it is not safe to evacuate or relocate.	• As Level 4 • No movement out of base/safe area, at any time, except to relocate/evacuate.

ROLES AND RESPONSIBILITIES

Every aid worker has a responsibility not only for their own personal security and safety, but for the safety and security of their colleagues and other agencies. Roles and responsibilities for safety and security must be identified in advance of a situation, in order to ensure a quick and effective response. All staff must be clear as to their given roles and responsibilities.

Shared responsibilities

Within Save the Children, roles and responsibilities for safety and security are divided into three categories: individual, management and organisational.

Individual

All Save the Children staff members are responsible for their own safety and security and should exercise common sense.

All staff are responsible for the safety and security of their fellow staff, along with Save the Children's assets, under their management and care; and should, when possible, reasonably support the safety and security of implementing partners and beneficiaries.

Irrespective of the organisation's assessment of risks in a particular situation, any staff member may decline to take up work in an insecure area, and has the right to leave the project or refuse to carry out particular duties if they feel their safety is in danger.[1] In some situations Save the Children may require staff to withdraw from an area, suspend operations, or temporarily close an office for security reasons. Such decisions are binding on all staff and should be acted upon with immediate effect.

All staff have a personal and professional responsibility to report to the Country Director or their line manager all safety and security incidents and any behaviour or actions by other staff members that either breach Save the Children's policies or compromise team safety and security in any way.

[1] Save the Children Safety and Security Policy and Standards – Standard 12, February 2010

[2] Save the Children Safety and Security Policy and Standards – Standard 1, February 2010

[3] Save the Children Safety and Security Policy and Standards – Standard 3, February 2010

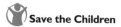 Save the Children

Your organisation's global security policy and the country-level safety and security plans should clearly define the responsibilities and obligations of all staff members in relation to staff security and safety – ie, individual and management responsibilities, the decision-making process, and how decisions are taken in relation to serious incidents affecting staff members.

Management

Each manager has a responsibility for the safety and security of the staff they manage.

The Country Director is ultimately responsible for safety and security management in the Country Office.[2] At a minimum, the Country Director is responsible for:

- Establishing and maintaining an effective safety and security management system that is compliant with Save the Children Safety and Security Policy and Standards.
- Monitoring security trends and the safety situation in country and the region in order to determine the appropriate security threat level at all times.
- Ensuring the Country Office has adequate budget provisions for safety and security-related expenses to maintain safety and security standards.

Each Country Office should appoint at least one Safety and Security Focal Point (SSFP) to support the Country Director and SMT in the implementation of safety and security management.[3] In higher-risk Country Offices a full-time Security Officer should be employed.

Regional/Area Directors are responsible for maintaining oversight of safety and security management within their respective countries and ensuring that Country Offices have the resources and capacity to manage safety and security effectively.

In the event of any serious incident, either directly or indirectly affecting a Save the Children staff member or the team as a whole, the Regional/Area Director and Head Office must be informed immediately. Depending on the nature and severity of the incident, coordination and decision-making may be undertaken at a senior level within Head Office, in consultation with the Country Office and the respective Save the Children members.

Organisational

The overall organisational responsibility for staff safety and security lies with the respective Save the Children's Chief Executive.

The respective Director of Global Programmes is responsible for monitoring policy implementation and advising Directors and the Board of Trustees on security matters. Permission to adopt practices that exceed the policy can be granted only by the Chief Executive.

The Global Safety and Security Department (GSS) provides guidance to Save the Children management on matters related to safety, security and crisis management, and supports initiatives designed to enhance the safety and security of personnel and operational activities. The GSS is responsible for:

- Establishing Save the Children policies, procedures and standards that will ensure the highest level of security for Save the Children staff and assets and the lowest risk of loss and liability to the organisation.
- Monitoring existing and potential risks to staff and programmes, and proposing measures to mitigate those risks.
- Developing and disseminating appropriate and effective security resources.
- Providing consultative services to Country Office Directors including: training, security assessments and staff support.
- Enhancing and maintaining Save the Children crisis management capabilities.

Further support and advice is provided at the regional level by the Senior Specialists for Regional Safety and Security (SSRSS).

2 PERSONAL SECURITY AWARENESS

Your personal security is first and foremost your own responsibility. You can't just rely on the security policies and plans put in place by your organisation; these are effective only to the extent that they are put into practice by each individual staff member. In any case, no amount of planning can anticipate all the problems that may arise.

It's essential that all staff develop awareness of their own personal security, and understand how their actions or inaction in a particular environment can jeopardise their own safety and that of their colleagues. Staff must understand how their conduct can damage the image and reputation of their organisation and its capacity to operate.

DEVELOPING AWARENESS

In its simplest form, developing awareness means paying attention to your surroundings and being alert to any changes. This is particularly important when you first arrive in a new environment, as your understanding of it will obviously be limited. Indications are that nearly one-third of all deaths of humanitarian workers occur in the first three months of duty.[*] It is vital to quickly develop a keen awareness of your environment and adjust your behaviour to take account of the risks you may be exposed to. When you are unfamiliar with a situation you may miss important subtle

[*] M Sheik, 'Deaths among humanitarian workers', *BMJ*, 321 (2000): 166–68.

changes that, if you were more aware, would indicate a threat to your security. You must be able to recognise these danger signs before they develop into a threat. If you can quickly notice changes in your environment or people's behaviour, you'll be able to take early action to minimise the risks.

Being unfamiliar with cultural dynamics may also expose you to unnecessary dangers; for example, if you naively behave in a way that antagonises a local group or individual. An understanding of the cultural norms and the different roles and restrictions for men and women will ensure that you behave appropriately, and it may lead to greater respect and concern for your safety from the local community.

Each national and international staff member has an obligation to develop personal security awareness. This means you must understand the locations and communities in which you are working. Although this learning curve will be steeper for international staff, national staff, too, should continue to develop their security awareness and apply it to what

---

Briefings and orientations

All Save the Children Country Office staff must be given an orientation on the safety and security policies and procedures, including their respective roles and responsibilities.* This core safety and security orientation should be provided within the first week of staff or others taking up duties.

All visitors (including dependants)/travellers to Save the Children Country Offices must be provided with pre-departure information and with a safety and security briefing within 48 hours, and for higher-risk countries within 24 hours, upon arrival in country.

* Save the Children Safety and Security Policy and Standards – Standard 4, February 2010

 **Save the Children**

---

they already know about the area. In order to develop your personal security awareness you need to act on the following recommendations:

- **Be briefed**. Before working in any area, ensure you are fully briefed on the security situation and informed about the mandate and principles of your organisation. Details on the general security situation should be given to you before you accept a position, so you can make an informed choice. A more detailed local security briefing should be given to you when you take up your position in the field. Briefings should include specific details on the overall political situation; the different conflict dynamics; the prevalence of crime; the humanitarian situation; and the key risks and security precautions necessary to deal with them.
- **Do some research**. In addition to the information you will be given by your organisation, it is important to do some independent research. Detailed information on the country, its culture, and political and security situation can be easily found on the Internet, in newspaper articles, and in various books and reports.
- **Speak to others**. Try to consult as many and varied people as possible. Talking to your colleagues, other agencies, and individuals in the community is the best way to develop a good awareness and understanding of the situation.
- **Stay alert**. Keep your eyes and ears open at all times. Be conscious of what is unusual or threatening. If you notice things are not normal (empty markets or quiet streets that are usually busy), then ask people why. Ultimately, trust your 'gut feelings'; if you feel threatened, leave the area immediately and find somewhere more secure.

DEVELOPING RELATIONSHIPS

Building a positive rapport and good relations with the people you work with is probably the most important contribution you can make towards your own security. Developing good relations can increase both your security awareness (because people may warn you to potential risks) and your overall protection (because a community that accepts and welcomes you may also attempt to protect you). At times of crisis, neighbours and colleagues are often the best protection you can have.

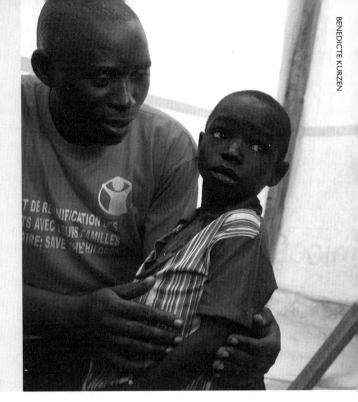

Developing good relations can increase both your security awareness and your overall protection.

In building positive relations it is important to consider the following:

- Interact as often as possible with your neighbours, communities, local staff, etc. Listen to them.
- Introduce yourself to and build a rapport with the local authorities and community leaders.
- Involve yourself in community activities apart from your work. Do not let your only interaction with the local community be when you enter and leave your protected compound. However, be aware of how any interaction you do have is perceived by others, as there may be security implications resulting from the relationships you develop.
- Attempt to learn the local language and practise it as often as possible.
- Avoid expressing political or religious opinions with people you do not know well.
- Avoid being drawn into relationships that might carry personal obligations or expectations you cannot meet.

BEHAVIOUR AND ATTITUDES

Many humanitarian organisations are driven by fundamental values and principles, and it's important that all staff uphold standards of behaviour that correspond to those values and principles. It is just as important to be conscious of the cultural sensitivities of the communities and colleagues you are working with. In some societies, certain behaviour and actions of staff may be viewed as inappropriate: for example, how they dress, with whom and how they communicate, and their personal relationships. In some contexts these issues may be gender-related; for example, female staff wearing short skirts or sleeveless shirts can be perceived as disrespectful to local codes and religious sensitivities. Male staff members who don't show composure and self-control in certain contexts may

Think carefully about how others see you, and how your actions or behaviour might be perceived.

also create resentment. Even if this behaviour doesn't result in a direct threat, it could heighten existing suspicions and tensions in the community.

Remember that at all times you are an ambassador for your organisation. Think carefully about how others see you, and how your actions or behaviour might be perceived. Avoid any behaviour and attitudes that might offend or provoke aggression. Your inappropriate behaviour may damage your agency's image and could expose not only yourself but also your colleagues to unnecessary risks.

To avoid giving offence or provocation, adhere to the following basic principles in your conduct:

- Communicate and interact with all individuals in a dignified and positive manner, according them respect as individuals and community members.
- Be respectful towards the religious beliefs, local customs and cultural practices of the communities in which you work. In situations where staff feel they must question customs and practices that are harmful to individuals, this must be done in a sensitive and appropriate manner.
- Do not participate in any form of abuse, violence or improper conduct that exploits anyone, especially those over whom you have a duty of professional trust or care.
- Strive to create an atmosphere of openness and mutual respect with your colleagues. Share information and include others in the decision-making process.
- Make sure you understand the ground rules in your location for personal communication between men and women; for example, acceptable levels of familiarity and how to greet male and female members of the society.
- Be aware that in some cultures it is unacceptable for female staff to work closely or travel alone with male colleagues. Consult with colleagues to find an acceptable solution; for example, ensure that two or more female staff travel or work together.
- Be considerate in your social and domestic behaviour. You may be living and working with colleagues from many different cultural backgrounds. It is important that team security is not jeopardised because of unnecessary or avoidable team conflicts.

- Make sure your dress indicates respect for the local culture and dress codes. Avoid displaying obvious signs of wealth, such as expensive jewellery.
- Do not possess or use illegal drugs or controlled substances. Be aware of local laws and attitudes; alcohol may be illegal, or at the very least public drunkenness may be frowned upon. Always refrain from excessive use of alcohol as this can compromise personal and team security.
- Sexual relationships between team members, or with individuals in the community, may be considered offensive to local laws and customs and could place the individuals involved and their colleagues or families

Code of conduct

As an employee or representative of Save the Children, **you must** promote its values and principles and protect its reputation by:
- Respecting the basic rights of others by acting fairly, honestly and tactfully, and by treating people with dignity and respect, and respecting the national law and local culture, traditions, customs and practices that are in line with UN conventions.
- Working actively to protect children by complying with Save the Children's child protection policy and procedures.
- Maintaining high standards of personal and professional conduct.
- Protecting the safety and wellbeing of yourself and others.
- Protecting the organisation's assets and resources.
- Reporting any matter that breaks the standards contained in Save the Children's Code of Conduct.

Maintaining high standards of personal and professional conduct means **you must not** behave in a way that breaches the code of conduct, undermines your ability to do your job or is likely to bring Save the Children into disrepute. For example, **you must not**:
- Engage in sexual relations with anyone under the age of 18, or abuse or exploit a child in any way.

at risk. The sexual exploitation or abuse of local people, especially beneficiaries, is not only morally unacceptable but also likely to increase risk to individuals.

- Do not demand or accept any personal favours of any kind from contractors or others providing services to your organisation. Always maintain a cordial but professional relationship with others related to your work.
- Do not misuse the financial or material resources of your organisation. Means of transport, equipment, and residential and office accommodation should be chosen and acquired to meet operational needs only. Ostentatious appearances will reflect negatively on you and your agency.

- Exchange money, employment, goods or services for sexual favours.
- Drink alcohol or use any other substances in a way that adversely affects your ability to do your job or affects the reputation of the organisation.
- Be in possession of, nor profit from the sale of, illegal goods or substances.
- Accept bribes or significant gifts (except small tokens of appreciation) from governments, beneficiaries, donors, suppliers or others, which have been offered as a result of your employment.
- Undertake business for the supply of goods or services to Save the Children with family, friends or personal contacts or use Save the Children assets for personal benefit.
- Behave in a way that threatens the security of yourself or others.
- Use the organisation's computer or other equipment to view, download, create or distribute inappropriate material, such as pornography.

Code of Conduct for Save the Children Staff,
February 2005

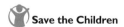 **Save the Children**

BASIC PERSONAL SECURITY MEASURES

The best way to deal with threats to your security is to avoid them in the first place. There may be exceptional security risks in the areas where you are working; while dealing with these, it's easy to forget basic personal security measures associated with travelling or working in unfamiliar environments.

When it comes to personal security, gender can be a significant factor, and one of the main reasons why different members of staff can experience different levels of risk while doing the same jobs in the same environment. For example, in many contexts male staff members face increased risks associated with violent confrontation and assault, and may be more at risk in terms of harassment by the authorities and security forces. Female staff are clearly more at risk than their male colleagues from sexual harassment and rape. While it is important that both male and female staff are aware of these additional gender concerns when it comes to their personal security, all the measures discussed here* are applicable to both male and female staff.

General measures

In everyday activities it's vital that you give careful consideration to the following basic personal security measures:
- Be aware of the specific security concerns in your location, and the procedures in place to deal with them.
- Trust your instincts. If you feel uncomfortable about a location or a situation, leave immediately.
- Always communicate your whereabouts and plans, or any changes to those plans, to colleagues.
- Make sure you are able to identify yourself if asked. Carry appropriate personal documents with you at all times. Make sure your passport, ID cards, visas and health certificates are valid.

* The measures described in the following nine sections are adapted from *Security in the Field: Information for staff members of the United Nations system*, UN, New York, 1998.

- Make sure you have a supply of emergency cash with you at all times.
- Always be aware of and respect any local curfews.
- Take care while using cameras or video equipment as these can raise suspicion. Do not take pictures near military installations, airports, governmental buildings, etc. Always ask permission from your colleagues or from local people before taking photographs.
- Avoid displaying cash or other valuables as this may attract attention from potential robbers.
- Avoid routines as they make your movements easy to predict. Be alert to anyone observing your house, office or travel routes. Vary routes to and from work and the time at which you take them. Many security incidents occur as an individual either leaves or returns home.
- If you are in any danger, try to draw attention to yourself by shouting, screaming or using the horn of your vehicle.

When travelling

When travelling to and from your field locations, consider the following basic precautions:

- Always check the security situation of the location to which you are travelling.
- Before travelling, leave your planned itinerary and contact details with a responsible person.
- Keep people informed of any changes to your travel plans and any delays.
- Be clear about your arrival arrangements and know who is meeting you.
- Check in advance with your field office what you should do in the event of a problem, or if there is no one there to meet you.
- Carry a list of emergency contact details including names, addresses, phone numbers, and the names of reputable hotels along your route.
- Look confident and dress appropriately, with valuables out of sight.
- Keep an eye on your possessions, particularly during security checks, in the baggage collection area and while clearing customs.
- If possible, take only licensed taxis or those recommended by your field office. In some countries taxi drivers are known to commit crimes or be accomplices. Agree fares before you get in, make sure you have the sole use and the driver will not pick up other passengers, and check that your bags are actually on board before you depart.

In hotels

If you are staying in a hotel or guest house, consider the following basic precautions:

- If making your own hotel arrangements, make sure the hotel has been approved by your field office. Advise your colleagues of your hotel location and room number.
- Avoid rooms on the ground floor, or any rooms that are easily accessible from the outside.
- Take note where the safety exits are in case of fire or any other emergency. Keep a flashlight by the bed.
- Keep a small bag packed and make sure important items are close at hand in case you have to leave quickly.
- Always secure the door when inside your room, using locks and security chains. Keep windows and balcony doors locked and draw the curtains.
- When not in the room consider leaving the light and television or radio on so it appears that the room is still occupied.
- Be careful of opening the door to callers (including hotel staff) unless they can identify themselves in some way.
- Consider the best way to deal with valuables and, if possible, obtain advice from your field office. Do not leave valuables in your room: leave them in a hotel safe deposit box, in a locked safe in the room, or carry them with you when you go out.

When driving

When driving in an unfamiliar setting, consider the following basic precautions:

- Always wear seatbelts and do not drive under the influence of alcohol or other intoxicating substances.
- Whenever possible avoid travelling at night. If this is not possible, avoid unlit and deserted roads.
- Keep the car windows closed and the doors locked.
- Do not drive alone, especially at night, and think about driving in groups or convoys – even for short distances.

- Be particularly alert when your car is stationary; for example, at a road junction or traffic lights.
- If you think you are being followed, make a few turns down busy streets to check. If you are, do not go into your own driveway or a deserted area, but drive to somewhere you know you can get help, such as the nearest police station.
- If someone tries to force you off the road, sound your horn to attract attention.
- At all times maintain an adequate distance between your car and the vehicle in front, to allow you space to manoeuvre and escape if necessary.
- Never pick up hitchhikers, and think twice about stopping to help what appears to be a stranded motorist, regardless of gender.

More detailed vehicle security measures are discussed in Chapter 6: 'Travel safety and security'.

On foot

In insecure or unfamiliar settings where you are required to walk, consider the following precautions:
- Be aware of your surroundings – do not put yourself into a vulnerable position.
- Seek reliable advice on safe areas. Do not take short cuts through isolated areas.
- Avoid walking alone, especially at night.
- Maintain a low profile and avoid any disputes or disturbances. Be wary of groups of people loitering on the streets.
- Make sure your bags are closed and securely carried to avoid them being snatched. Valuables should be concealed under clothing or in a front pocket.
- Cross the street if someone suspicious is walking behind or ahead of you. If you are still being followed, head to a populated area and attract the attention of others.
- Carry only the cash that you need. Keep a small amount of cash in your wallet to hand over in the event of being mugged. The remainder should be divided between your pockets and bags.

- Avoid carrying your passport unless it is required as identification.
- If a driver pulls up to ask for directions, do not approach the vehicle. Be cautious when asked to look at a map. If you are offered a lift, politely refuse.

Using public transport

If you are using public transport, consider the following precautions:
- Travel in pairs whenever possible.
- Wait in well-lit designated areas during off-peak hours.
- Avoid travelling in deserted trains or buses. If possible, sit near the driver or conductor. When travelling by train try to select a lockable compartment.
- Be careful when accepting any food or drink as it may be drugged.
- After getting off, check to ensure you are not being followed.

In your home or temporary residence

While in your home or temporary residence, consider the following basic precautions:
- Be sure to keep your doors and windows locked, even when you are at home or leaving the building for only a few minutes.
- Keep curtains or blinds closed at night.
- Avoid sleeping with your windows open unless they are protected by bars or grilles. Keep valuables and possessions away from open windows, even if they are protected by bars, as it is common for items to be 'fished' through openings.
- Be wary of unexpected visitors, especially after dark. Identify all visitors before opening the door.
- Carry only the keys that you use, and mark them so you can identify them quickly in the dark.
- If you find that a door or window of your home has been broken open while you were out, do not go in. Leave quietly and summon help.

More detailed residential security measures are outlined in Chapter 5: 'Site safety and security'.

In social situations

When in a social situation, consider the following basic precautions:
- Take care when meeting someone you do not know well; choose public places or places where there will be other people present.
- Avoid drinking too much, as this will limit your ability to notice and react to changes in people's behaviour.
- Be careful when accepting any food or drink as it may be drugged.
- Communicate your wishes clearly. Do not let anyone assume unwanted intimacy.
- Assert yourself and insist on being treated with respect.

Sexual harassment

Sexual harassment should not be tolerated in any context. Any unwanted and offensive conduct, verbal or non-verbal, which is targeted at an individual because of their gender, can constitute sexual harassment. The conduct itself does not have to be sexual in nature and can be directed at either men or women. Be aware that what you may consider in your own culture to be 'friendly contact' might be perceived by others as culturally unacceptable sexual harassment.

Sexual harassment can take a multitude of forms. You may be the target of sexual harassment from a random stranger while walking in the street, or from a colleague while in the workplace or a social setting. Some common forms of sexual harassment include:[*]
- obvious sexual gestures or remarks directed at you
- staring at your body
- repeatedly asking you out for a date
- uninvited visits to your room
- sending you lewd or pornographic emails or pictures
- close physical contact
- subtle or unsubtle pressure for sexual favours
- threats of physical assault.

[*] Adapted from *Be Safe Be Secure: Security Guidelines for Women*, UNDSS, New York, 2006.

If faced with any unwanted attention, you may consider any one or more of the following steps:

- Ignore the advances. If the person is just trying to get a reaction from you and they find that they can't, they may stop.
- Confront the harasser. Talk to the person directly if you feel comfortable and secure in doing so. Explain that their behaviour makes you uncomfortable and you find it offensive, and ask them to stop.
- Tell someone. Discuss the problem with a friend, colleague or someone you trust. Get advice from appropriate sources on how to handle it, and on the options available.
- Document the harassment. While the incident is still fresh in your mind, write down what happened, where, when, and how you responded. Include names of any witnesses.
- Report the problem to your manager or another senior member of staff. Those responsible for the security and welfare of staff should always take allegations of sexual harassment seriously.

3 STAYING HEALTHY

It's an unfortunate fact that during your work you are very likely to be exposed to many causes of ill health. The environments and working conditions in which aid workers have to operate often involve high workloads, traumatic events, cultural challenges, hostile climatic conditions, basic living conditions, poor dietary options, and inadequate hygiene and sanitary facilities. Such circumstances clearly create a high risk of ill health, be it through illness, injury or stress. You need to remain constantly aware of your personal health, so that you can stay physically and mentally healthy.

WHO IS RESPONSIBLE FOR HEALTH?

The simple answer to this question is *yourself*. Knowing what the risks are, and how to avoid them, is the key to staying healthy. You have a responsibility to yourself – and your fellow team-mates – to ensure that you fully understand the health risks that exist where you are working, and that you take the necessary precautions to avoid illness or injury. When a staff member is ill, it doesn't affect them alone: in serious cases it can have a major impact on the other team members and the programme.

LOOKING AFTER YOURSELF

In areas of armed conflict, gunfire, landmines and shelling obviously represent a serious risk to life. In truth, however, in many countries malaria, diarrhoea and traffic accidents present a far greater risk. Looking

Staff medical cover

Save the Children provides medical cover for international employees and their recognised accompanying dependants.* Cover includes medical costs in the country of posting or nearby country, repatriation costs, and medical costs in the country of domicile where no free treatment is available. There are restrictions and conditions to this cover.

Save the Children also accepts responsibility for the healthcare of nationally appointed employees. The extent of this care depends on local circumstances, the availability of medical care, and the conditions of employment. Save the Children's International Staff Health Policy should be used as good practice guidance to enable each Country Office where Save the Children operates to develop its own policy on staff health for national staff. Save the Children is guided by People in Aid and other sector-specific experts on staff health provision.

All international employees are given advice and information about health issues during their induction. At country, regional and Head Office levels, human resources professionals and line managers can give advice on how best to access information on health matters. Further information can be obtained from the International Staff Health Toolkit through the Save the Children Intranet.

In-country, Country Directors are responsible for the healthcare of employees. They must ensure that appropriate medical facilities are found to give healthcare and support in the first instance.

* Save the Children's Policies International Staff: Medical Provision, July 2009

 Save the Children

3 STAYING HEALTHY

after yourself isn't just confined to the period when you're working in the field. Most staff will stay healthy if they make careful preparations before they travel, and pay attention to the advice they are given. It's also important to take adequate care of yourself after, as well as before and during, your assignment.

Preparation

Before travelling, whether it's for a short trip or a long-term placement, you need to consider the following:
- Be aware of the key health risks in the area in which you will be working.
- Make sure you know what health insurance and medical evacuation cover has been arranged for you in case of emergency.

In many countries malaria, diarrhoea and traffic accidents present a far greater risk than violent conflict.

Medical checks

Save the Children requires that all international staff and their recognised accompanying dependants undertake a medical check before employment.* Staff are requested to complete an Adult Health Screen (pre-employment medical). In-country/regional Human Resources will ensure correct forms and advice are available to international staff at job offer stage and when considering travel.

* Save the Children's Policies International Staff: Medical Provision, July 2009

 **Save the Children**

- Check with your doctor all necessary immunisations that are required, and allow enough time to complete the course.
- Obtain and take with you any certificates that may be required – eg, for yellow fever. Note that some countries require an HIV-free certificate.
- Seek medical advice as to which antimalarial you should be taking if travelling/working in a malarial zone. Take sufficient antimalarials, repellent and a mosquito net. Make sure that you start your course of antimalarials at the recommended time before departure.
- Know your blood group and keep a written record with you.
- Make sure you take enough of your regular personal medications with you, with any additional medicines you are likely to need.
- Discuss any health concerns with your organisation's staff health adviser and/or a doctor.
- Consider having a dental and eye check before travelling.

While working in the field

Each country presents its own health risks to individuals. On arrival in the field it's essential that you're fully informed about the key health issues that exist for that location. In order to maintain a good state of health while working in the field you must be aware of the following:
- Make sure you fully understand the health provision that's been made available to you. Provision could include: pre- and post-employment

medical screening, insurance cover for non-routine medical and medical emergencies, routine medical cover, and psychological support/counselling.

- Maintain your awareness of health risks that exist, either in the country as a whole or in particular locations you'll be visiting.
- Take your antimalarials as prescribed if working in a malarial zone, and do not stop taking them before the recommended time after leaving a malarial zone.
- Make sure you keep your immunisations and immunisation records up to date.
- Ensure that you have a safe/clean source of water. Use water filters if necessary.
- Take care to maintain a healthy lifestyle: ie, a nutritious diet, sufficient fluids, limited consumption of alcohol and tobacco, adequate rest and manageable working hours.
- Ensure that you know how to contact the relevant people in an emergency. Be familiar with your organisation's medical emergency procedures.
- Be aware of the health facilities available locally. If possible, register with a local doctor or clinic in-country, and have their contact details in case of an emergency.
- Report any illness and injury to your team-mates or line manager as soon as possible. Minor illnesses or injuries can be potentially dangerous if not treated properly, so make sure you seek advice. More serious cases should be reported to your organisation's staff health adviser.

Post-assignment

Looking after yourself does not end the moment you finish your assignment. It's essential that you continue to look after your health on your return home. You need to consider the following points:

- If available, undertake a post-employment medical and psychological assessment provided by your organisation to discuss any concerns or health-related issues.
- Visit your own doctor and ensure that you have a medical check on your return, ideally with a travel health specialist.

3 STAYING HEALTHY

- Continue to take your antimalarials as prescribed after leaving a malarial zone.
- Take an adequate break before your next assignment.

FIRST-AID KITS

Each agency site and all vehicles should be equipped with a basic first-aid kit. The contents of these kits will depend very much on local circumstances. However, it's important to note that first-aid kits do not save lives by themselves; only people who know what to do and when to do it can save lives. In some circumstances it's worth considering taking personal first-aid and syringe kits. Personal first-aid kits contain simple items for self-treatment in case of minor illness or injury. Syringe kits contain sterile syringes and suturing materials for use by medical personnel only. Seek advice as to the need for personal first-aid kits in your location.

First-aid kits

Save the Children does not provide standard first-aid kits for all staff.* All Save the Children offices, residences and vehicles should have basic first-aid kits. The contents of these kits will vary according to local circumstances: ie, known health risks and availability of facilities locally.

Responsibility for assembling and maintaining first-aid kits must be clearly delegated to one person. The Global Safety and Security Department can provide advice on the appropriate contents of the kits.

* Save the Children Safety and Security Policy and Standards – Standard 8, February 2010

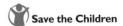 Save the Children

---

MEDICAL EMERGENCIES

A serious injury or sudden illness may mean you need immediate medical or hospital treatment. In medical emergencies such as these it's important that you and your colleagues know how and where to get the best medical attention.

When local medical assistance or hospital treatment is unavailable or inadequate, an individual may require medical evacuation ('medevac') to a reliable medical facility in-country, in a neighbouring country or in their home country. For most organisations, medevac to another country is available only for internationally recruited staff. In the event of a medevac, established procedures must be followed to ensure a swift evacuation and prevent delay in the provision of medical care.

Your agency's medical emergency policy and procedures must be clearly understood by all staff, to ensure a safe and efficient response to medical emergencies. Local medical emergency plans should include information about the following:

- Who is responsible for staff health and medical evacuation procedures in the field, and who takes over the responsibility in their absence.
- Contact details of a doctor in-country who will assist staff in a medical emergency.
- Local healthcare institutions that could be used in an emergency, with a brief description of the facilities available and their limitations.
- The nearest hospital of international standard, with a brief description of the facilities available and any limitations.
- The nearest air access points (plane/helicopter) that could be used in the event of a medical evacuation, including length and type of airstrip, seasonal implications, use at night, fuel availability, etc.

Medical emergency procedures

All Save the Children international staff and their recognised accompanying dependants are covered by Save the Children's emergency medical and evacuation insurance.* All staff must be fully aware of Save the Children's medical emergency procedures, as any deviation from these procedures could invalidate Save the Children's insurance cover for the staff member involved.

In all cases the respective HR Manager should be consulted on any condition that is causing concern and which may not be an apparent medical emergency.

Full details of medical evacuation procedures are available from the respective HR Managers and the Global Safety and Security team. Further information is also available through the Intranet.

* Save the Children's Policies International Staff: Medical Provision, July 2009

 Save the Children

COPING WITH STRESS

Stress factors in the world of humanitarian aid are very different from those you may normally face in your home environment, and at times they can seem overwhelming. First, there are practical issues such as adapting to a new environment, different cultures, language and food. Then there are work factors such as long hours, frustrating bureaucracy and, at times, security fears. You may be separated from your partner, family and friends, living with team-mates on top of each other as a group, or isolated from them in a remote programme. Added to this is the potential for witnessing inhumanity and suffering for long periods of time. Any one or an accumulation of these factors is bound to affect you in some way.

If stress is allowed to build up to an unacceptable level it can make people ill, create disharmony within a team, and even disrupt the entire programme. How teams and individuals cope with stress will depend on the culture and nature of the people concerned. It's essential to recognise that you and others are likely to be affected by stress, if it is to be effectively managed.

Stress factors

Stress is a normal reaction in abnormal situations. As time passes you will generally adapt to your new environment and working conditions, and the stress will normally subside. It's worth remembering that not all stress is negative: for example, some people feel they're more productive when

Stress factors in humanitarian aid can seem overwhelming – long hours, frustrating bureaucracy and security fears are bound to affect you in some way.

stressed by an important deadline. Stress helps you focus your attention on the situation or task in hand, mobilises the energy you need and prepares you to react. Therefore, stress can be positive in terms of your safety and security in a tense or risky situation.

But stress is physically and mentally draining, and can be dangerous when it occurs too often, is too intense or lasts too long. Continually being exposed to stress factors such as work pressures, difficult living arrangements and insecurity, without sufficient time to recover, will weaken your defences. Cumulative stress will eventually take its toll on your health and can lead to physical and emotional exhaustion or 'burn-out'.

Traumatic stress is caused by direct experience of, or close exposure to, a sudden, unexpected and violent event. Experiencing a life-threatening incident or witnessing a traumatic event causes severe stress and can have a major impact on your physical and emotional wellbeing. Reactions to traumatic stress will vary from one individual to another, and symptoms may appear immediately or a few hours or days later. Post-traumatic stress may present itself months or even years after the event.

Recognising the signs of stress

In order to deal with stress it's important to be able to recognise it in yourself and others. Note, however, that recognising the signs of stress in yourself is difficult, as it often affects your ability to think clearly. Stress can take many and varied forms, and it may bring physical, emotional and behavioural changes.

Dealing with stress

Aid work can never be stress-free, but what is stressful to one individual can be a positive stimulus to another. The key to dealing with stress is recognising the factors that can cause *you* stress, and where possible identifying practical coping mechanisms that will enable you to manage it.

Signs of stress

Physical effects	Emotional effects	Behavioural changes
• Disrupted sleep • Fatigue • Headaches • Cold sweats and/or trembling • Skin problems • Nausea, with or without vomiting • Increased heart rate and blood pressure	• Depression, low self-esteem • Negative attitude and cynicism • Feelings of anguish and guilt • Anger and irritableness, seeking to attribute blame • Nightmares, flashbacks • Excitable, feeling heroic and invulnerable	• Excessive working, inability to let go or delegate • Poor work performance, absenteeism • Poor concentration, confusion • Indecisiveness, inconsistency • Increased alcohol and/or cigarette intake, drug abuse • Self-neglect in terms of appearance and hygiene • Aggressiveness, angry outbursts • Risk-taking, dangerous driving • Social withdrawal, poor communication with colleagues and family

Source: Adapted from *Humanitarian action and armed conflict: Coping with stress*, ICRC, Geneva, 2001.

Working environment

Humanitarian work is demanding, and some goals set by organisations or individuals are not always attainable. It is important to maintain realistic expectations of what can be achieved in the field in order to avoid the 'headless chicken' syndrome: people running around, believing they are achieving a lot but in fact getting nowhere. Make sure you get a good briefing and clear job description, and that you know your objectives and what's expected of you. Discuss these expectations with your manager and if possible define achievable goals.

Try to avoid long hours in the office. Because of insecurity, or limited social activities, there is a tendency for aid workers to work long hours. However, it's important to maintain as far as possible a normal structured working day, and to ensure that you set aside sufficient time to relax – even if it sometimes means that important work has to be put off until later. Someone who is exhausted or 'burnt out' is of little value to an organisation, and may even be a liability to their colleagues.

Living environment

Group living creates additional stresses, owing to the lack of privacy and the inability to switch off from day-to-day work problems. Try to ensure you have some private space to unwind and relax, whether to read, listen to music or simply do nothing. Take time to make your living arrangements comfortable, as a relaxing atmosphere will help you to unwind and recover from the daily stresses.

Stress places great demands on the body so it's vital to maintain good physical health, through regular exercise or by undertaking activities that help keep you physically fit. Make sure you sleep well and maintain a healthy diet. Try to control your intake of alcohol, cigarettes and caffeine, as these stimulants only give a superficial sense of relaxation and excessive use will cause additional stress to your body.

Away from work it's important to use free time constructively. Take part in social activities that enable you to interact with friends and colleagues, and try to talk about things other than work.

Leave

It's essential that you get reasonable and regular breaks away from your working environment. There's a tendency to delay leave because of work pressures or insufficient staff cover, but it's important that staff take their leave when it's due. In difficult working conditions – for example, an emergency or a highly insecure environment – additional leave may be required.

Additional support

Discussing concerns with others is a crucial part of dealing with stress. However, in the absence of friends or family this can sometimes be difficult. Try to identify someone you trust, either within your team or organisation or even from outside, with whom you feel you can share your concerns and who will listen and, if need be, offer constructive advice.

If either you or a colleague are showing signs of severe stress, particularly in the case of traumatic stress, it's important to seek additional professional support.

Staff support

Save the Children will make additional support available to any national or international staff member who needs assistance while working in the field. In these cases the Country Director will enlist the help of local counselling services, if they exist.

For international staff a 24-hour telephone helpline is available to give immediate advice and guidance;* the Human Resources Manager in-country will be able to advise staff of how to access this support. Further information can be obtained directly through the International Staff Health Toolkit, available through the Intranet. If staff require confidential specialist counselling support, they should contact either their Regional HR Manager or Global HR.

* Save the Children's Policies International Staff: Medical Provision, July 2009

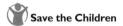 Save the Children

4 WORKING IN CONFLICT ENVIRONMENTS

The environment in which humanitarian agencies operate has changed dramatically in the past decade. With the end of the Cold War and the subsequent shifts in global, as well as local, power relations, the world saw an unprecedented number of violent internal conflicts and civil wars. Today, the vast majority of conflicts are internal and are fought in and around communities, resulting in large-scale population movement and huge numbers of civilian casualties. Most contemporary conflicts pit government forces and associated militia and paramilitary groups against insurgents of various kinds. These insurgents may be motivated by ideology, ethnic or religious identity, political grievances or the pursuit of economic gain. There are often several different groups operating at any one time with little to distinguish civilians from armed actors involved in the conflict.

In order to gain and maintain access to beneficiaries, humanitarian agencies are often forced to negotiate with many different armed actors. These groups have a variety of mandates and styles of discipline, and many have no knowledge of or – worse – flagrantly disregard international humanitarian norms and agreements. For aid agencies, operating in such complex environments and knowing how to interact with the various armed actors are two of the most challenging aspects of the current humanitarian landscape.

In recent years, there's been a sharp increase in deliberate attacks against aid workers operating in certain conflict environments. Having lost some of the protection that was afforded to humanitarian agencies in the past, aid agencies are now sometimes perceived as representatives of

Knowing how to interact with the various armed actors is one of the most challenging aspects of the current humanitarian landscape.

international governments, or their assistance as part of a wider political or military agenda. In such environments, associating with the military or certain armed actors – however indirectly or unavoidably – could exacerbate these perceptions and ultimately jeopardise the security of you and your colleagues.

DEALING WITH ARMED ACTORS

The presence of military forces and other armed elements is fairly common in many humanitarian emergencies. It's essential that, as an aid worker, you develop a good understanding of the context, the nature and causes of the conflict, and the different actors involved. The range of armed actors that you may come across when working in the field is very broad and may include the national military contingents, local police, local militia or paramilitaries, rebel factions or insurgency groups, criminal gangs, armed civilians, multinational/coalition forces, UN peacekeeping troops, international military observers, and private security companies.

In most situations aid workers will be required to establish some level of communication with different armed actors, either to negotiate access to affected areas and beneficiaries, or to ensure that the agency's mandates, roles and responsibilities are fully understood. The levels of interaction between your agency and the various armed actors will vary, and may be influenced by the perceived legitimacy and structure of the specific armed actors, how accessible they are and how they are regarded by others. When dealing with any armed actors it's important to adhere to the following guidance:

- **Keep a healthy distance**. While it's important to develop a relationship with all key actors in a particular environment, contact with armed actors should be kept to a minimum.
- **Keep it formal**. All interactions with armed actors should be calm, courteous and formal. Where contact does occur you should ensure that it doesn't compromise your independence or neutrality, or jeopardise the security of staff and beneficiaries.
- **Know who is who**. Fully research the armed actors or individuals you're dealing with and attend any meetings with a clear idea of what you're trying to achieve as well as the limitations of what information you can share.
- **Be respectful of the chain of command**. All armed actors, no matter how disorganised they appear, will have some form of chain of command and identifiable leaders; you should afford these leaders the same courtesies as you would when dealing with the national armed forces. This can be very difficult when you know they have committed atrocities. If engaging with a highly centralised armed group, engage at a senior level. With loose armed groups you may have to engage at all levels.
- **Explain your activities**. Armed actors will often be suspicious of your intentions and you must take the time to appear transparent and explain your activities to them in an attempt to gain their acceptance.

ENGAGEMENT WITH THE MILITARY

Since the early 1990s, there has been a trend during military interventions by the international community towards undertaking relief operations or quick impact projects (QIPs) in an effort to win the 'hearts and minds' of local communities. Military forces consider these kinds of initiatives to be of crucial value to protecting their forces and, more broadly, to the stabilisation of the country. The humanitarian sector is concerned about this blurring of lines between humanitarian and military activities.

Aid is becoming more politicised, and even militarised, and this may be placing aid agencies and their staff at additional risk.

Increasingly, humanitarian agencies may be perceived as working with or being part of a military force, which has serious implications for humanitarian space and how agencies operate in these environments.

Contributing to this dynamic is the evolution of integrated missions, combining the efforts of defence, diplomacy and development. This approach aims to ensure that aid, reconstruction and development projects are closely linked to a wider political and military agenda. For humanitarian agencies this raises concerns that aid is becoming more politicised, and even militarised, and that the lack of clear separation between humanitarian and military activities means that the image of aid agencies working in these environments is severely compromised. The

---

Engagement with armed forces

In determining any relationship between Save the Children and armed forces, Save the Children is guided by the UN Inter-Agency Standing Committee (IASC) Guiding and Operating Principles on Civil–Military Relationships and Use of Military Assets.[*]

Some degree of interaction and dialogue may be necessary, and in exceptional circumstances use of military resources may be considered. However, Save the Children must maintain its independence of decision-making and action, and must ensure that any relationship with the military or the use of military resources does not negatively affect the organisation or the safety and security of humanitarian personnel and beneficiaries.

Any action to engage with armed forces or make use of military assets must be authorised by the Country Director in consultation with the respective Regional/Area Director and the Director of Global Programmes.

[*] *Civil–Military Guidelines & Reference for Complex Emergencies,* Inter-Agency Standing Committee/UN OCHA, 2008

obvious worry is that this may be placing aid agencies and their staff at additional risk.

It's essential for aid workers to ensure that they and their programmes are not, and are not *perceived* as being, identified in any way with military or other security forces. However, staff will need to interact with military or other security forces in the course of their work, and there are a number of legitimate reasons why humanitarian agencies may seek to engage with the military:

- **To inform**. Establish communication links to inform the military of your agency's mandate and current activities.
- **To advocate**. Remind the military of its duties under international humanitarian law and highlight any humanitarian concerns that arise from the military's presence or its activities.
- **To obtain security information**. Information-sharing may be critical to the safety and security of staff and the overall relief effort.
- **To seek assistance**. Agencies may seek evacuation support, emergency medical care and mine clearance. Although the military should not be the first choice in a humanitarian agency's contingency planning, it may be necessary to seek specific emergency assistance, and to make use of the logistics resources available to the military; in which case, you'll be unlikely to get emergency help from the military if you haven't already established some kind of dialogue with it.

If you do engage with the military, it is vital that this doesn't undermine the neutral, independent, charitable character of your agency and its work, and that it doesn't lead to other actors in this context developing a negative view of your agency.

USE OF MILITARY ASSETS

The use of military assets to support humanitarian activities should always be a last resort and not undertaken without serious consideration of its wider implications. This is particularly the case in countries affected by armed conflict and civil unrest, and where the assets belong to a party in the armed conflict. However, in exceptional circumstances the scale of humanitarian need can be so great that aid agencies don't have the logistical capacity to respond effectively on their own, and the military is able to mobilise significant resources and manpower. In the wake of natural disasters, agencies generally are more ready to work with military forces. In these cases they may decide to use, in the short term, military or civil defence resources, as long as certain important principles are met:[*]

- **Last resort.** The use of military assets may be considered as a last resort, when no other civilian options are available to support the provision of humanitarian assistance in the time required.
- **Civilian control.** Use of military assets in a humanitarian operation must retain a civilian nature and character. Coordination should remain, if possible, under civilian control; humanitarian agencies must avoid operating under the command of the military, as this violates the core principle of independence.
- **Support role.** Humanitarian assistance should be delivered only by humanitarian organisations. Military assets should be used only to support humanitarian agencies and should not be used for direct assistance, in order to retain a clear distinction between humanitarian and military stakeholders.
- **Mitigating action.** Where military assets are used by aid agencies they must be clearly distinguished from those used for military purposes. For example, all weaponry should be removed, surveillance equipment uninstalled, personnel should wear civilian clothes and be unarmed, military insignia should be covered and the agency emblem displayed.
- **Short term.** The use of military resources must be limited in time and scale and there should be a clear exit strategy, and a strategy for achieving a civilian response in the future.

ARMED PROTECTION

Use of armed guards or escorts to protect staff and property is a more delicate issue, and one which many agencies are uncomfortable with. The basic principle for most agencies is NO armed protection. However,

[*] Civil-military Guidelines & Reference For Complex Emergencies, IASC/UNOCHA, New York, 2008.

The basic principle for most agencies is NO armed protection. However, there have been a number of extreme situations where agencies have used armed protection.

there've been a number of extreme situations where agencies have used armed protection; for example, in Somalia, Kenya, Iraq and Chechnya. Use of armed protection is an emotive subject and one on which agencies hold different opinions. It's an extreme strategy which can have a marked effect on a humanitarian agency's image. In some situations, such a strategy may actually increase your insecurity, by escalating the violence and increasing the risk that firearms may be used against you. One of the first questions you must ask yourself, if considering armed protection, is why do you need it? Have you crossed the threshold of acceptable risk? If the security situation warrants the use of armed protection, can you operate safely? If staff are clearly at risk, should you consider withdrawing or suspending your operations?

Exceptional measures

Save the Children only considers the use of armed protection in exceptional circumstances under strict criteria.[1] If a Country Director deems it appropriate to use armed personnel for protection of Save the Children premises, assets or other purposes (eg, armed guards at premises, armed escorts for travel), approval must be sought from the Director of Global Programmes or equivalent with the concurrence of the Head Office Safety and Security Focal point.

[1] Save the Children Safety and Security Policy and Standards – Standard 7, February 2010

 Save the Children

Any decision to use armed protection needs to focus on three key areas:[2]

- **Is it acceptable in principle?** Consider whether your organisation accepts the principle of armed protection. Does it recognise situations in which armed protection is necessary? Is it willing to pay for armed protection?
- **Is it appropriate in the context?** Look at the appropriateness of armed protection in the context in which you are operating; for example, what are the threats for which armed protection is needed? Will the use of armed protection actually reduce these risks? Is it the only or best solution? Who will provide the armed protection and what are the implications?
- **Are you able to manage it?** Consider issues of management; for example, do you have a detailed agreement or contract? Are there criteria for selection of guards or escorts in terms of training and experience? Who is responsible for supervision? Who is responsible for providing equipment and transportation, etc? Are there clear rules of engagement, or local laws, that determine when the guards or escorts will use force? Who is liable in case of injury or death?

[2] Adapted from K Van Brabant, *Operational Security Management in Violent Environments*, Good Practice Review 8, ODI, London, 2000.

5 SITE SAFETY AND SECURITY

A secure and safe environment is essential in order to operate effectively. It's vital that you feel protected and safe, whether you're working in your agency's office, distributing supplies in a refugee camp, or relaxing in your home. Ensuring a secure and safe environment requires careful thought and planning, regarding both the choice of site and the procedures and measures you adopt to maintain security and safety.

Remember that the site you choose and the security measures you adopt can affect the image and profile of your agency. Effective security measures must balance the need for physical protection and deterrence on the one hand, and the need for widespread acceptance on the other. In some situations, rigorous site security measures – for example, high walls, razor wire and armed guards – may be necessary to deter violent criminals. In others, this fortress mentality and how it is perceived could undermine acceptance of an agency's activities by the wider community.

Your choice of site and the security procedures you adopt can also affect your ability to operate effectively. Rigorous security procedures, even though warranted, are time-consuming and can restrict operations. In practice you will have to find a balance between a number of considerations. Perfect choices seldom exist. Consider the positive and negative impacts of potential sites and security measures, in terms of the level of protection they will afford, the operational impact, how you will be perceived, and the security strategy of your agency.

Ensuring a secure and safe environment requires careful thought and planning, regarding both the choice of site and the measures you adopt.

SITE SELECTION

In order to meet their operational requirements, agencies often need to occupy several different types of structures (offices, residences, warehouses). As well as the operational criteria concerning location, space and price, facilities must be assessed in terms of safety and security risks to staff and/or assets and supplies. Effective site selection involves making a thorough risk assessment first of all.

When assessing the location of a potential site you must carry out the following:

• Investigate levels of crime in the area, the types of incidents that have occurred and whether agencies in that area have been targeted before.

- Establish whether the site is located near other agencies' facilities, as there may be an increased risk in being more isolated.
- Check if the area or property is affiliated with a particular group, as this could either increase the security risks or provide a level of protection.
- Determine whether the site is close to potential targets – eg, government buildings or military installations.
- Determine whether the site is in close proximity to potential areas for demonstrations or civil unrest – eg, markets, religious buildings, universities, diplomatic areas.
- Consider distances and routes between the site and your other structures (residences, office or warehouse) as there may be security risks associated with moving between these sites.
- Examine how accessible the site is – ie, whether access is restricted or open to the general public. Check that there are multiple access routes to facilitate evacuation from site in an emergency.

As well as considering the risks associated with a particular location, you must evaluate the physical structures of the site for security and safety. Key areas to explore include:

- **Structures**. Assess the physical condition and strength of the buildings. Also consider their susceptibility to any likely hazards (fire, flood, strong winds, earthquakes).
- **Perimeter**. Examine the boundaries of the site, make sure there is a well-defined boundary, and that perimeter walls or fences are secure.
- **Access**. Inspect the condition of doors, gates and windows. Ensure all have adequate locks.
- **Lighting**. Make sure that the site is well lit, particularly access points and the street area outside the site.
- **Safety issues**. Check the condition of key services such as electricity, gas and water supply. Ensure that appliances are safe and that electricity sockets and wiring are in good order. Consider possible escape routes in the event of a fire.
- **Vehicle parking**. Vehicles are valuable assets and therefore are a prime target for thieves and vandals, and in some cases are the subject of sabotage. It is important to have a secure parking area, ideally within the compound, to avoid the need for parking vehicles on the street.

Before signing any lease or contract, make sure you have clear permission to carry out alterations to the site in order to improve security. You may need to discuss these alterations in advance and agree with the owner the work that will be done, who is responsible for undertaking it, and costs involved.

Once you've selected your site, you need to continually assess and re-evaluate its suitability in light of possible changes in security. Sometimes, if the security situation deteriorates, it may be necessary to change the location of where you live or work.

SITE PROTECTION MEASURES

Finding an appropriate site is clearly only the first step. Depending on the security situation, your selected site, or existing sites, will need additional protection measures and procedures to improve security. It is useful to think from the perspective of a criminal or potential attacker and identify weak points, either in the physical structures of the site or in the procedures you have in place. Having identified potential weak areas, consider what additional measures you can take to reduce the risks.

Perimeter security

Consider the additional measures that are required to improve the security of the site's perimeter. Remember that 'perimeter' does not only refer to the outer perimeter, ie, compound walls and gates, but to the inner perimeter, ie, windows, doors and locks of the buildings.*
Additional perimeter security measures could include the following:
* Clearing or trimming vegetation around the perimeter, particularly large overhanging trees that can be used to scale walls, or bushes that can be used as hiding places.

* J Davis, *Site Security: Security Training Module for NGOs*, OFDA/InterAction, 1998.

- Increasing the height of the compound wall to at least 2.5 metres, making it more difficult to scale. Otherwise, consider using broken glass or other materials on top of the wall to deter intruders. Look at the walls of other compounds to get an idea of the sorts of protection measures used locally.
- Strengthening the main gate. Solid metal gates are stronger and more difficult to scale, but need greater structural support. A chain-link gate can be scaled more easily, but provides a clear view of the area outside the perimeter.
- Creating an emergency exit in addition to the main gate to enable staff to leave quickly, in case of a violent mob breaching the main gate. However, this emergency exit must not create an additional weak point.
- Providing additional lighting around the perimeter to make it more difficult for intruders to use the cover of darkness. However, be careful not to upset your neighbours by having bright lights shining into their property all night. Sensor lights are good as they light up only when someone approaches.
- Strengthening the main doors to key buildings. Main doors of residences should have safety chains, peepholes and dead bolts installed inside.
- Fitting bars or grilles over the ground-floor windows. Ideally, grilles should be hinged so that in the event of a fire it is still possible to exit the property through the window.

Secure facilities

All Save the Children Country Offices, including residences and living compounds, should have a well-defined boundary, with secure perimeter walls or fences as appropriate. All exterior doors and windows should be secure, and access points should be well lit.*

* Save the Children Safety and Security Policy and
Standards – Standard 6, February 2010

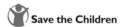 **Save the Children**

Access controls

All Save the Children Country Offices, including residences and living compounds, must have effective controls and procedures in place to manage access.* For higher risk or complex field offices, a guard force should be employed, either through direct hire or by using the services of a reputable contractor.

* Save the Children Safety and Security Policy and Standards – Standard 6, February 2010

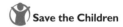 **Save the Children**

Managing access

A secure perimeter will be ineffective if criminals can simply walk through the front door. You must carefully manage staff and visitor access to your office, residence or warehouse. The degree of security control needed will depend on the general security situation, the type of property, and the security strategies you adopt, but when you are planning access controls, give careful consideration to the following basic security measures:

- All staff should carry photo ID cards. These must be collected from the staff member upon termination of contract/employment.
- All keys to the building should be tightly controlled. Stolen or lost keys should be reported immediately, and locks changed.
- All visitors should show identification before entering. All visitors should sign in and out, and if possible be given a visitor's pass that they should wear while on the premises.
- All staff must monitor who comes and goes. Any unknown visitor should be asked who they are and their purpose on the property, if staff feel it is safe to do so. Otherwise they should notify the guards or the manager.
- Services and delivery staff should not be admitted without proper identification and authorisation.
- Designate an area for use by waiting visitors, clearly visible to guards and/or reception staff.
- All visitors should be accompanied while on the premises.

Stringent access controls can be time-consuming and frustrating for staff and visitors, and therefore there is a tendency for staff to become relaxed about procedures over a period of time. All staff should be clearly briefed not only on the procedures, but on why such controls are needed. It's essential that all staff adhere to access controls; seniority should not exempt any staff member from following the procedures.

Guards

Use of unarmed guards and watchmen is commonplace at agency offices, residences and warehouses worldwide. The principal aim of such measures is to deter unauthorised or unwanted visitors from gaining access to an agency's property. In order for these guards to be effective, due care and attention should be paid to the conditions under which they are recruited and subsequently managed. There are a number of important issues to consider, including:

- **Guard selection**. As they occupy such a key role in your security, it's important to give as much time to selecting guards as you would a project manager. Try to find out about their background and seek reliable references, even if guards are provided by a private security company. Ideally they should be physically fit, but in some contexts seniority can be more effective. Make sure you employ enough guards, particularly at night. Guards will fall asleep, so you need to allow for this.
- **Agreement/contract**. Make sure you have a clear agreement/contract and job description for the guards. Due care and attention needs to be paid to issues such as additional responsibilities, what to do and who to inform in case of a security incident, and consumption of substances (alcohol or drugs) while on duty.
- **Equipment**. Be clear about what essential equipment you will provide: for example, flashlights, batteries, raincoats, boots, whistles, radios and shelter.
- **Training**. Make sure guards are trained to deal with, and to sign in, different types of visitors (officials, job applicants, beneficiaries, and other agency staff).
- **Engagement**. Provide clear instructions on how you wish the guards to engage if the compound is attacked, or if they find an intruder. You need to be clear on the appropriate use of force.

Shelters and barriers

In situations where there's a risk of staff being subject to direct or indirect small-arms fire, bomb explosions, shelling or aerial bombardment, additional site protection measures should be taken. Realistically, no shelter can be built by you that can protect against a direct hit from a shell or bomb, but the following measures can limit the effects and should therefore be considered:

5 SITE SAFETY AND SECURITY

- **Window reinforcement/blast film**. Flying glass fragments as a result of the blast will be the cause of most injuries. It's possible to limit the impact of the blast by covering windows with wooden planks or shutters. Although expensive, the other option is to fit blast or shatter-resistant film on windows. Blast film aims to keep panes of glass together, even after it has shattered, therefore reducing the amount of glass fragments flying around. There are a number of ways to fit blast film, each of which has implications for effectiveness, safety and cost, so it's important to seek further advice.
- **Blast walls**. Blast walls are designed to shield occupants from small-arms fire and a nearby blast. Sandbags can be used to build a blast wall, but this must be constructed properly so that it does not collapse, and should be at least above head height. Blast walls can be placed externally in front of windows, doors and other weak points, or can be used internally to provide additional shelter.
- **Shelters/safe room**. Shelters are designed to withstand a larger blast, but will still not withstand a direct hit. As the best protection is afforded underground, a cellar can provide very good shelter. Make sure that shelters are adequately ventilated and protected from flooding. You may well have to strengthen the roof of the shelter; this can be done with strong wooden beams. In the absence of any underground shelter, identify the strongest room on the ground floor, often a small room such as a bathroom or cupboard with small or no windows and less roof span.
- **Trenches/foxholes**. Trenches strategically placed in the compound can provide immediate protection from mortar shells and aerial attack. Trenches must be at least two metres deep, but narrow. Placing sandbags around the edge of the trench can provide additional

protection. These trenches must be regularly maintained, as heavy rains can cause them to collapse, and they tend to be a great place for snakes to hide.

One obvious danger with these kinds of protective measures is that they can lull staff into a false sense of security. Again, it's important to ask yourself whether your organisation can really operate effectively in an environment where such precautions are necessary.

FIRE SAFETY

The importance of fire protection is often overlooked. Fire poses a significant risk to aid workers, especially in countries where there is no fire brigade, buildings are not built to minimise fire hazards, and few people have fire-safety training. Fires in offices, warehouses and residences can prove catastrophic, and the threat of fire should be addressed in all risk assessments. While most fires start small and can be extinguished if detected early, the best method for fighting fires is prevention – through regular inspections, staff training and properly maintained fire-fighting equipment in all facilities.

Basic fire safety precautions

When considering site protection measures, it's vital to ensure that the following fire safety precautions are followed:
- Store fuel as far from any office or residence as possible. Make sure that the store is secure, ventilated and shaded, and 'DANGER, NO SMOKING' signs (in the relevant languages) are clearly visible.
- Smoke detectors must be fitted in all residences and offices, and must be tested regularly.
- Make sure that appropriate fire extinguishers and blankets are available, in sufficient quantity, and that all staff know how to use them. Remember, NEVER use water on electrical, oil or petrol fires – either it will electrocute you (in the case of electrical fires) or it will cause an explosion.

- Identify fire-escape routes. In large buildings it's important to run fire drills regularly to ensure that staff know how to evacuate the building safely, and that they are aware of the meeting points.

Fires in buildings

Fires can spread very quickly, trapping people inside the building. It is important to react quickly. If you discover a fire in your building:

- Alert others so that the building can be evacuated as rapidly as possible. Operate the fire alarm or shout a warning.
- Ensure that others are aware of the problem, waking them up if necessary.
- If the fire is small, and you've been trained to extinguish fires, try to do so, tackling it with appropriate extinguishers. However, don't put yourself or others at risk and always operate in pairs in such a situation. Remember – if you can't extinguish a fire by the discharge of a single extinguisher, then it may be better to get out.
- Stay low while moving. Smoke kills more people in fires than flames or heat. Get down as low as possible, as there will be more air and less

---

Fire protection

Appropriate fire-fighting equipment must be installed in all Save the Children Country Offices, including residences and living compounds, and the equipment should be regularly maintained.[*]

All Country Offices, including residences and living compounds, must ensure that emergency exiting procedures are established with agreed gathering points. Staff should receive regular fire safety training and fire drills should be conducted quarterly.

[*] Save the Children Safety and Security Policy and Standards – Standard 6, February 2010

 Save the Children

5 SITE SAFETY AND SECURITY

smoke at floor level. A damp towel wrapped around your nose and mouth will allow you to breathe more easily.
- Check closed doors for heat before you open them. There may be a fire on the other side that will flare up when the door is opened. Close doors behind you as you escape.
- Use the stairs, if in a tall building. Do not take the lift.
- If you cannot leave the building, seal all cracks with wet clothes; switch off fans/air conditioners. Keep all doors closed between you and the smoke of the fire.
- If your clothes catch fire, stop, drop and roll over and over to smother out the flames; running only makes the fire burn faster. If someone else is on fire use water, sand or a fire blanket to smother the fire while they are rolling.
- Once you are safely out of the building, *stay out.*

FIELD SITE SECURITY

As agency staff will spend a significant amount of their time working in the field (for example, distributing supplies in a refugee camp or providing medical services in a healthcare centre), it's vital to give appropriate consideration to the security of these sites. In addition to site security issues already outlined, field sites have their own specific security concerns. The presence of valuable commodities and essential services will often attract large crowds and heighten expectations. If the population feel the distribution is not fair, or if they have to wait a long time for services, their frustration may result in outbreaks of violence. This can lead to increased security risks to staff and resources, as well as to the beneficiaries themselves.

When working at a field site, you need to take the following basic precautions:
- Be alert and maintain awareness of your surroundings at all times.
- Proactively seek out information on what's happening in and around the camp. Be informed of any potential problems and disputes.

- Become familiar with the layout of the camp or health centre. Know where other agencies are working, and the location of authorities, police and military.
- Locate your field base/camp office near the main access routes and, preferably, at the edge of or away from the camp.
- Keep others aware of your movements while on site. Always carry your radio and inform your base of your movements and, if relevant, inform camp authorities or other agencies when you arrive and leave the site.
- Never walk through the camp alone; always travel with someone else.
- Try to avoid any disputes. If disputes over resources and services arise, try to channel discussions through appropriate representatives, and do not get drawn into any argument.
- Consider how you would evacuate the site in the event of insecurity. If a number of agencies are working in a camp, make sure you are aware of the evacuation and emergency communication procedures, meeting points and evacuation routes.

CROWD CONTROL

In tense and confusing situations, a purely peaceful gathering can easily turn aggressive and violent, resulting in the looting of agency assets and supplies and, in some cases, aggression against agency staff. Crowds can get out of control if people are confused about, or unhappy with, what is happening. There may even be organised forces at work deliberately stirring up feelings. Of crucial importance when dealing with any large crowd is awareness, careful planning and coordination. It's important to give careful consideration to the following basic crowd-control measures:
- Never encourage a crowd to gather unless you can meet their needs or answer their concerns.
- Ensure that clear information is provided to the community in advance.
- Meet with community leaders and representatives to work out procedures and discuss concerns.
- Organise people into smaller groups. If distributing aid, consider having a number of distribution points to discourage large crowds

Staff will spend a significant amount of their time working in the field, it's vital to give appropriate consideration to the security of these sites.

from gathering. Ask the community leaders to assist with crowd control and seek their advice on the appropriateness of 'official' crowd control measures – eg, the presence of police or recognised authority.

- Inform the crowd what will happen and, if necessary, show them the series of events that will take place. For example, during some food distributions, representatives are shown exactly what individuals will receive at each stage of the distribution process.
- Consider the crowd's physical needs: shelter, water and sanitation. If people have to wait for long periods of time, encourage them to sit, and provide waiting areas with shade.
- Use representatives of the community as crowd-control staff.

- Establish a mechanism whereby individuals can air their grievances. If possible, have separate staff and community representatives to deal with these issues away from the main crowd, to cause less disruption.
- Do not engage in disputes directly, but channel discussion through community representatives. Do not become angry and, if necessary, try to defuse the situation by showing that you are willing to discuss the issues further with a smaller group of representatives away from the main crowd.
- Plan evacuation of staff from the area in the event of a breakdown in crowd control, and a threatening situation arising. Keep a vehicle nearby and ready to leave.
- If you are in a vehicle and are confronted by a crowd, do not get out. Lock doors and carefully drive away from the situation.

Of crucial importance when dealing with any large crowd is awareness, careful planning and coordination.

6 TRAVEL SAFETY AND SECURITY

In many countries, the greatest risks to staff occur during routine travel and movements, either while travelling in the field or moving to and from the office. Ambushes, shootings, carjacking, abductions, landmine incidents, vehicle accidents and other incidents while on the road account for the majority of safety and security incidents affecting aid workers.[*] This indicates just how exposed and vulnerable you and your agency's assets are while in transit.

In insecure environments, vehicles are an essential tool for avoiding potential danger. However, in some situations they can actually be the cause of insecurity. An aid agency vehicle and its occupants can be an easily identifiable target for those who want to vent their anger against a particular organisation, or against humanitarian agencies in general. The new and expensive vehicles often used by agencies can also make them an ideal target for criminal groups.

While most staff travel and movements involve the use of vehicles, in some situations staff have to use air transport or boats to travel long distances or to reach communities in isolated or inaccessible areas, and these often present additional risks to staff. The establishment of, and adherence to, effective travel and movement procedures is essential in order to minimise the safety and security risks associated with all staff movements.

[*] A Stoddard, A Harmer, A and K Haver, *Providing Aid in Insecure Environments: Trends in Policy and Operations*, ODI, London, 2006.

In many countries, the greatest risks to staff occur while travelling in the field.

JOURNEY PLANNING AND PREPARATION

Preparation and planning is the key to safe and secure travel. Many of the safety and security incidents staff face while travelling are the result of inadequate preparation and planning. When planning a journey it's important to consider the following guidelines:

- **Know the area**. Be aware of the general security situation and the safety and security risks that may exist. Keep abreast of any military developments and identify locations or areas to avoid. Identify the various agencies working in the vicinity or in the areas en route.
- **Study the route**. Find out as much as possible about the road conditions, consult with other agencies and organisations to monitor route conditions, and change routes as necessary.

- **Avoid routine**. In areas with criminal activity or other known threats, consider alternative routes and timings. Avoid developing routines. Keep your journey plans confidential.
- **Plan for delays**. Estimate the time of arrival for different points along the route and plan your journey to arrive at your destination well before nightfall. Anticipate possible delays and calculate them into your journey times.
- **Check and prepare vehicles**. Vehicles must be checked before any journey. Ensure that they are in good condition and have all the necessary equipment and supplies; for example, spare wheel and tyre-changing tools, spare fuel, tow rope and first-aid kit.
- **Documentation**. Ensure that all documentation needed for travel is with the vehicle, including vehicle registration, road tax, insurance, permission to travel, radio licence, waybill for supplies, etc, as required. Drivers and passengers should carry personal identification (ID card, passport or photocopy) and relevant driver's licence.
- **Communications**. Establish communication procedures for monitoring vehicle movements. For example, agree the frequency of communications and/or the specific communication points along the route. Ensure that all passengers know how to use the communication equipment and who to call in an emergency.
- **Contingency plans**. Contingency plans should be developed in case of problems. For example, you should identify alternative routes and safe locations in case of insecurity, and establish procedures in the event of losing communications.
- **Submit a journey plan**. It's important to notify others of your travel plans, times, destination and route. Plans should include steps others should take if you do not arrive as scheduled.

VEHICLE SAFETY

It is well reported that traffic- and vehicle-related accidents are among the major causes of injuries and fatalities for aid agency staff. It's a sad fact that many of these accidents could have been avoided, if basic guidelines had been drawn up and followed. In both secure and insecure areas, vehicle safety is a basic principle that should be adhered to by all staff. The guidelines should cover:

- **Safe driving**. The combination of poor road conditions, challenging terrain and powerful vehicles is an ideal recipe for accidents. Safe driving means recognising the limits of your vehicle and the risks the environment poses, and adjusting your driving accordingly. This skill is not inherent in all drivers, and therefore safe-driving training is a necessity for all.

- **Speed**. All vehicles are difficult to control at high speed, particularly four-wheel drive (4WD) vehicles. It's important to establish clear speed limits, both in built-up areas and on open roads. Vehicles must be able to stop quickly and safely in an emergency, and therefore should only be driven at a speed at which the vehicle is stable, regardless of set speed restrictions. Safe speed limits must be rigorously enforced.

- **Seat belts**. The wearing of seat belts is compulsory. Not only is it a legal requirement in many countries, but there is statistical proof that it reduces the impact of a vehicle accident. Only on very rare occasions should it be judged appropriate not to wear seat belts; for example, when wearing them might critically hinder staff who need to escape from their vehicle quickly.

If you are carrying supplies or equipment in vehicles, you should ensure that all cargo is packed and secured appropriately so that it can't cause injury to the driver or other passengers.

VEHICLE SELECTION

Your choice of vehicle(s) can have a significant impact on safety and security. When selecting vehicles you should consider the following issues:

- **Type of vehicle**. There is an array of choices to be made: 2WD *vs* 4WD; diesel *vs* petrol; passenger vehicle *vs* pick-up. Operational needs may have to be weighed against safety and security implications. In many environments, sturdy 4WDs may seem the safest choice, but could be the more likely target of criminals. Diesel vehicles are more economical

Effective travel and movement procedures are essential in order to minimise safety and security risks.

Vehicle travel

All Save the Children vehicles, including rental vehicles, must be equipped with the appropriate safety equipment (first aid kits, fire extinguishers, seat belts, etc). It is mandatory for drivers and all passengers to wear seat belts and for helmets to be worn by all motorcyclists and any passengers.[*]

[*] Save the Children Safety and Security Policy and Standards – Standard 8, February 2010

 **Save the Children**

and have a low fire risk, but are more difficult to maintain and use in very cold climates. Long-wheelbase vehicles are more stable off-road than short-wheelbase vehicles or pick-ups. It is important to determine what you need the vehicle for and what impact your choice may have on staff safety and security.

- **Tyres**. Tyres must be appropriate for the road conditions – ie, Tarmac, on-off road, mud or sand – and they must have good tread depth. You need to consider whether tyres should be tubed or tubeless, as tubeless tyres cannot be fixed easily by the side of the road, so are not recommended for use in remote areas.
- **Visibility**. New white 4WD vehicles are highly visible. This visibility can be either positive or negative in terms of security. Consider the nature of security threats in your location. In areas where there is a risk of becoming caught in sudden crossfire you may want to enhance your visibility by using vehicles that are distinct from those used by the general population. In other situations – for example, where carjacking of agency vehicles occurs – you may consider adopting a lower profile by using locally rented vehicles.
- **Condition of vehicle**. Reliable vehicles are essential for safety and security. Vehicles must be roadworthy, not a death trap. Do not select a vehicle that is likely to break down when you need it most.

SERVICING AND MAINTENANCE

All vehicles operating in the field should be mechanically sound and properly equipped. It's important that vehicles are regularly serviced and maintained to ensure reliability and minimise breakdowns. A worst-case scenario is a vehicle breaking down in an insecure area as it gets dark or while staff are trying to evacuate. Regular servicing and maintenance schedules must be in place, whether it's a case of one vehicle or a whole fleet. It's the drivers' responsibility to make sure that the vehicles meet these schedules and that the information is recorded in the vehicle log book.

VEHICLE POLICIES

All staff should have a clear understanding of their agency's position on a variety of vehicle-related issues, such as who is permitted to drive, the carrying of non-agency personnel, and weapons in the vehicle. All of these issues have clear safety and security implications.

Driver policy

Vehicles should be driven only by drivers specifically employed by your organisation, or by other staff officially authorised to drive. All drivers should hold valid driving licences for the country or region concerned. Many organisations permit only locally recruited drivers to drive their vehicles. This is considered preferable because these drivers have greater knowledge of the area, are familiar with the environment, and speak the local language, which can help passage through checkpoints, etc.

Some organisations do permit international staff to drive, particularly in large cities where they consider the security threats to be minimal. This can have implications for insurance cover. The decision as to who is allowed to drive and in what circumstances will be dictated by the local context and associated risks, but you need to have a clear policy on this.

Passengers

Carrying passengers in an agency vehicle implies responsibility on the part of the agency for the protection and security of those passengers. In an insecure environment this issue can be especially difficult. You must be clear about your agency's position on carrying non-agency passengers in your vehicles. For example, are you permitted to carry a local government employee to a field site? Where it is necessary to transport non-agency personnel, you should seek authorisation from senior management and obtain it in written form.

In an emergency, however, it may be necessary to carry injured or sick people to a hospital or medical facility. In such cases the injured or sick

Driving policy

It is Save the Children's policy that only Save the Children employees are allowed to drive vehicles owned by Save the Children. The right to drive is further limited to those staff members who:

* Have passed a driving test appropriate to that type of vehicle and have written authorisation from the Country Director to drive Save the Children vehicles.
* In the case of international staff, have a valid driving licence in their home country, and also (if required by local law) either a valid international or local driving licence, both licences being appropriate to size and type of vehicle.
* In the case of local staff, have a valid local driving licence appropriate to the size and type of vehicle, if local legislation/ mechanisms exist for such licensing.

All Save the Children employees and hired drivers driving Save the Children-owned/hired vehicles must confirm in writing before first being authorised to drive a Save the Children vehicle that:

* They have read and agreed to adhere to Save the Children Vehicle Policy (including the key rules from Save the Children Driver's Handbook) and the Code of Conduct.
* They are eligible to drive the type(s) of Save the Children vehicle that they intend to use under the terms of these rules.
* They will obey all local laws applicable to them as users and drivers of vehicles.
* They know how to change a wheel.

Save the Children's Drivers' Handbook,
January 2010

 **Save the Children**

6 TRAVEL SAFETY AND SECURITY

should be accompanied by a family member or official carer. Where possible you should notify the hospital or medical facility in advance that you are coming, in case of problems en route.

In all cases it's vital to consider who you are transporting, how it will be perceived by others, and how that may affect your own security, or that of your colleagues.

Arms on board

For most agencies it is a fundamental principle that NO firearms or weapons should be carried in their vehicles. Only in extreme security situations would armed protection in an agency vehicle be permitted.

No involvement with arms

Save the Children adheres to the principle that no armed personnel, firearms or weapons of any type are permitted within its vehicles, unless the proper approval procedures have been followed to allow protection of Save the Children staff and property.[*]

[*] Save the Children Safety and Security Policy and Standards – Standard 7, February 2010

 **Save the Children**

DRIVER MANAGEMENT

Drivers play a central role in vehicle use and movements. They have a responsibility for the safety and security of their passengers, as well as their obvious responsibilities for looking after the vehicle. Drivers are your eyes and ears in many situations. They often act as interpreters, are required to negotiate access through checkpoints, and can be the public face of your organisation for some of the local community. Therefore, drivers can directly affect the image that local people and authorities have of your agency. It's essential that you give sufficient thought to, and plan carefully for, their recruitment, roles and responsibilities, briefing and training.

Recruitment

When recruiting drivers, you must assess more than their abilities in safe driving and vehicle maintenance. You must also consider matters such as temperament (their ability to deal with threatening situations); age and status (an elderly driver may gain more respect and prove more resourceful in dealing with authorities and checkpoints); and ethnicity (the ethnicity of the driver could have either a positive or a negative impact on their own and their passengers' security).

Roles and responsibilities

It's important to define the roles and responsibilities of drivers in relation to vehicles and movement procedures. These must be clearly communicated to all drivers. Issues that must be covered will depend on local circumstances, but might include:

- **Vehicle checks**. Vehicles must be well maintained and also kept clean. Drivers must report vehicle defects and ensure that the vehicle log book is completed. Drivers must be provided with full details of what the daily and weekly vehicle checks should include.
- **Documentation**. Drivers are ultimately responsible for ensuring that all vehicle and travel documents are in order and that they are in the vehicle before departure.
- **Safe driving**. Drivers are responsible for ensuring that vehicles are utilised safely. The use of seat belts is compulsory in all vehicles at all times and speed limits are to be observed. It is ultimately the responsibility of the driver to ensure that these safety rules are enforced.
- **Vehicle refuelling**. Drivers are responsible for fuelling their vehicle(s) and must be informed about when and how vehicle refuelling is carried out. For example, they must ensure that vehicles have a full tank at the end of each day in case of emergency evacuation.

- **Parking**. Drivers must be instructed on how vehicles should be parked, both during office hours and during the night. For example, at night vehicles should be parked facing the exit to facilitate speedy departure from the compound if required.
- **Breakdown and accident procedures**. In the event of a vehicle breakdown or accident, drivers should be aware of what to do and who to inform.
- **Security incidents**. Should a security incident arise, drivers should be clear about how to behave, what to do and what not to do, and who to inform, to minimise the effects of an incident.
- **Grounds for dismissal**. It should be clearly explained to drivers what constitutes unacceptable behaviour, which would form grounds for dismissal. For example, consumption of intoxicating substances (alcohol or drugs); theft; negligence resulting in an accident; and use of a vehicle for personal or commercial purposes.

Briefing and training

Drivers, like all other staff, are representatives of your organisation. It is vital that they can accurately communicate to others the mandate and mission of your organisation. Drivers employed by the organisation, and drivers of locally hired vehicles, should all be briefed not only on their roles and responsibilities, but on the organisation and its programme activities.

As a significant number of security incidents occur during travel, drivers are particularly vulnerable. It is essential that drivers receive security training in addition to any driving skills training. Training should focus on key issues such as vehicle checking, safe driving, checkpoints, convoy driving, and crisis handling.

VEHICLE MOVEMENT PROCEDURES

To maintain safety and security during vehicle movement, you must have clear procedures in place that are understood and adhered to by all staff. Vehicle movement procedures will undoubtedly have to be adapted to suit the local context and the specific threats that exist. These procedures should provide general advice on movement as well as guidance on specific issues such as dealing with vehicle accidents, checkpoints and travelling in convoys.

Basic precautions

Basic precautions should be taken during all vehicle travel and staff movements, even in areas that are relatively secure. Basic precautions include the following:

- **Be alert at all times**. Always expect the unexpected.
- **Continually gather information**. Seek advice on the road ahead and the security situation from local people, bus drivers, transport companies, officials (including police and military) and other agency staff you meet along the route.
- **Avoid travelling alone**. On long or high-risk journeys a driver should be accompanied by at least one other person. Where possible, vehicles should travel in convoy rather than alone (see below on travelling in convoys).
- **Avoid travelling at night**. In areas where night driving is known to be dangerous, all journeys should be planned so that you arrive at the final destination in plenty of time, allowing for possible delays.
- **Be prepared**. Where there is a known risk (carjacking, landmines, ambushes, roadblocks, etc), ensure that all vehicle occupants know how to react if an incident arises (for further information see Chapter 9: 'Dealing with security threats').
- **Maintain communications**. Check that communication equipment is working and keep others regularly informed of your movements.
- **Safe driving**. All drivers should respect local traffic regulations, particularly where curfews, checkpoints (see below) and speed limits are concerned.

- **Know what's in your vehicle**. Be aware of what items are in the vehicle. Make sure you have appropriate documentation for all items and supplies being transported.

Checkpoint procedures

Checkpoints are often viewed as a security threat. To some extent this is true, as you may have to engage directly with threatening individuals who are likely to be armed. But not all checkpoints pose a threat; in some cases they can provide reassurance and be a source of information on the security situation in the area. In insecure environments they are a legitimate way for the authorities to observe and control movements. Security threats that do arise tend to do so because checkpoints are manned by personnel with varying degrees of experience, education, or training. In many countries checkpoints are manned by young, underpaid (if paid at all), frustrated and frightened soldiers. Often they may feel more at risk than you. This can make the situation tense and, if not handled carefully, it can easily spin out of control. It is vital to regard all checkpoints with caution, and be cooperative, patient and polite.

Although not all checkpoints pose a threat, it is vital to regard checkpoints with caution, and be cooperative, patient and polite.

IRIN NEWS (WWW.IRINNEWS.ORG)

Guidelines on dealing with checkpoints will vary depending on the context. What may be customary in one location may be unacceptable in another. It is important when arriving in a new situation to find out about the different types of checkpoints, what they look like, who mans them and the accepted procedures. As a general guide you should consider the following:

- **Assess the situation**. If you see a checkpoint ahead, quickly assess the situation. If it feels suspicious, stop some distance away and covertly report the situation by radio to your base. Decide whether to proceed or turn back.
- **Approach slowly**. When approaching the checkpoint always slow down. At night, dip your headlights, and switch on the interior light.
- **Turn radio down**. Turn down (or off) all radios in the vehicle and wind down the driver's window so that any order to stop can be clearly heard.
- **Stop if asked**. You may not need to stop, but if you are ordered to, or there is some form of barrier, stop the vehicle. If there is more than one vehicle, keep a reasonable distance between vehicles. Keep the engine running unless you are ordered otherwise.
- **Identify who is going to speak**. Make sure in advance that everyone is clear on who should speak and what they should say. Everyone should know the purpose of the journey and what, if anything, is being carried in the vehicle. Be aware that conflicting remarks can create suspicion.
- **Be ready to answer questions**. Answer all questions as accurately and courteously as possible. Do not raise any objection to identity or vehicle checks. There is no point in arguing with the people manning the checkpoint as they are probably acting under orders.
- **Stay inside the vehicle**. Do not get out of the vehicle unless ordered to do so. Keep hands visible at all times.
- **No sudden movements**. Do not make sudden movements as this could be misinterpreted. If necessary explain what you are going to do first.
- **Stay calm**. Use judgement about protesting if you are denied access or items are removed or confiscated. Do not aggressively resist if something is taken. Request documentation if possible. After the event report any abuses by those at checkpoints to the local authority.

- **Avoid bribes and gifts at all times**. Do not offer goods in exchange for passage. This can make it more difficult for your agency, or others, to pass through the same checkpoint the next time.
- **Inform base**. Once through the checkpoint and when at a safe distance, report clearance of the checkpoint by radio to your base.

It's important to be aware that there have been many instances of criminals posing as police or soldiers and setting up illegal roadblocks in order to rob vehicles that stop at them. If you come across an unexpected roadblock, be very wary of it. If necessary, and if possible, turn around and go back the way you came.

Vehicle accident procedures

The possibility of vehicle accidents can be limited by safe driving, but of course they cannot be avoided entirely. If you are involved in an accident it's important to handle the situation correctly. If mishandled, it can quickly change from an unfortunate accident into a security risk. In extreme situations it can trigger violence or threats of retribution. The following procedures should be followed to mitigate the effects of an accident.

- **Assess the situation**. Quickly discern the attitudes and behaviour of people around the accident site to ensure that you and your staff are not at risk.
- **Stop or not?** Do not leave the scene of the accident unless your safety or that of your colleagues is jeopardised, and then only to move to the nearest police station or military post. Make sure you are briefed on how you should respond to a vehicle accident in your particular country as the advice will vary from country to country.
- **Provide assistance**. If someone is injured, provide immediate care and assistance as appropriate and if further assistance is required take them to the nearest hospital.
- **Report it**. Make contact with your base/office and report the incident. If appropriate, contact the police immediately and cooperate as required.
- **Remember insurance**. Adhere to procedures required by your insurance company with regard to vehicle accidents. If feasible,

take photographs of the scene and record the names and contact information of those involved, witnesses, and responding authorities.

- **Do not discuss compensation!** If issues regarding settlement to victims for death or injury, loss of livestock or vehicle damage arise, get advice from senior management

When approaching an accident involving other vehicles, consider the safety and security of your vehicle's occupants before responding.

Travelling in convoys

In insecure situations, convoys are sometimes used to move personnel and supplies from one location to another, in order to reduce security risks. Convoys can range from a couple of agency vehicles travelling together to a fleet of trucks transporting food. Depending on the circumstances, the convoy may be officially escorted (armed or unarmed). The principle of this 'strength in numbers' approach is to deter criminal attack by making it more difficult for them to hold up and rob a number of vehicles at once. Vehicles travelling in convoy can also provide assistance to each other in the event of an accident or breakdown. However, large convoys are highly visible and can provide a large and slow-moving target for hostile forces. Your decision to travel by convoy will be dictated by the types of threats that exist locally and by what or whom is being transported (supplies, personnel or beneficiaries).

In addition to the basic guidelines for vehicle movement, if you are travelling as part of a convoy you are advised to consider the following:

- All convoys should have a leader who is responsible for the management of the convoy.
- Where possible, plan the route in advance, determining estimated times of arrival for each stage of the journey, and designate stopping places. Leave a journey plan with your base.
- Consider alternative routes and prepare contingency plans in the event of an accident or medical emergency. Expect vehicle breakdowns, and have agreed procedures for dealing with them.
- When necessary, notify local authorities of movements to allay

suspicion. In some circumstances authorisation from the relevant authorities may be required and a detailed travel plan submitted. Share travel plans on a need-to-know basis only.

- Prepare a full list of the convoy vehicles, including registration details and names of drivers assigned to each vehicle. Take care to decide on the position of each vehicle in the convoy, depending on the number and types of vehicles and the cargo and resources they are carrying.
- Make sure that all the vehicles in the convoy are in good condition and have the necessary equipment and supplies for the journey.
- A convoy can only move as fast as the slowest vehicle. Prior to departure the convoy leader should reject any vehicle that is not up to the journey or that he/she feels may slow down the convoy to the extent that security is threatened.
- Once the convoy is on the move, maintain radio communication between vehicles, particularly the lead and control (rear) vehicles, and with the field base.
- Do not drive too fast. Maintain an agreed steady speed. Do not overtake other vehicles in the convoy.
- Maintain a constant distance between your vehicle and others. Decide in advance the distance to be maintained between vehicles – this depends on the terrain, the speed required and the amount of dust being thrown up – and stick to it. Drivers should always be able to keep sight of the vehicles immediately in front of and behind them.
- Decide beforehand what to do if the convoy is obstructed. If required to turn back, reverse all vehicles until it is safe for them to turn around and drive away, starting with the last vehicle first.

AIR SAFETY

While air travel is generally regarded as a safe and reliable means of transport, in some countries there is increased risk due to extreme weather conditions and terrain, limited infrastructure and poor safety standards. Recent fatal air crashes around the world clearly highlight the dangers associated with air travel in many of the regions and countries in which aid workers operate.

*While air travel is generally safe and reliable,
in some countries there is increased risk.*

In general, the risk is best managed by choosing reputable airlines and
routes that present the lowest risk. However, in some countries and
regions the choice of carriers that fly to the airports required by aid
agency staff is limited. While information and flight safety records on air
operators is available on the Internet, the safety ratings given to airlines
often apply to the company as a whole and there might be considerable
differences between their international and domestic operations. In
addition, it's not only the airline's safety record and maintenance practice
that will affect the risk, but the condition, management and equipment
of the airports the carrier uses. Therefore, in countries where there
are concerns regarding the safety of certain air operators, you should
undertake further enquires and consult other organisations to help you
evaluate the risk associated with flying against the risks associated with
alternative means of travel.

Basic air safety precautions

When flying in a country or region where there are doubts about air safety, minimise the risk by adhering to the following basic precautions:

- Where possible avoid airlines with a known poor safety record. If you have concerns about the general safety of the proposed flight, speak to your line manager.
- If possible, avoid routes with stopovers, as most accidents occur during take-off and landing. The fewer stops you make, the less risk you face.
- Take account of seasonal and local weather conditions in your travel planning. Excessively bad weather or a forecast of such weather should be considered good reason for delaying your journey.
- When checking in, request an aisle seat nearest the emergency exits. The over-wing exits have less drop distance to the ground than those away from the wings.
- Don't board a flight if you have serious safety or security concerns, such as too many passengers for the number of seats; it is clearly overloaded with baggage and/or freight in the aisle; or poor security screening in an area where there is a risk of unlawful interference during the flight.
- When you board, always familiarise yourself with the location of exit doors and hatches and how to operate them.
- Check that your seat has a working safety belt and lifejacket. If not, move to another seat.
- Always report any incidents or safety concerns you encounter during travel to your line manager.

Travelling by helicopter

Helicopters are often used in major relief operations in order to gain access to areas where fixed-wing aircraft cannot land, or where the road infrastructure is badly damaged. However, travelling by helicopter poses an additional safety hazard and it's vital that you understand how to approach and leave a helicopter safely. In addition to respecting instructions from pilot and ground staff, when travelling by helicopter the following basic safety measures should be adhered to:

- Never enter the landing area without first obtaining the permission of the ground staff, or receiving the pilot's visual acknowledgement.
- When you do approach or leave a helicopter, always keep in the pilot's field of vision. *Never* approach or leave a helicopter from the rear.
- Do not approach or leave a helicopter when the engine and rotors are running down or starting up.
- The tail section of the helicopter is particularly dangerous. The tail rotor can be hypnotic and people have been known to walk or run into them. Do not duck under the tail boom – always walk around the front.
- If you need to approach a helicopter with the rotors turning, only do so when signalled by the pilot. Proceed in a crouched manner to ensure extra clearance, as blades can flex down. The most dangerous time is when the blades are turning slowly and the wind is gusty.

Helicopter safety zones

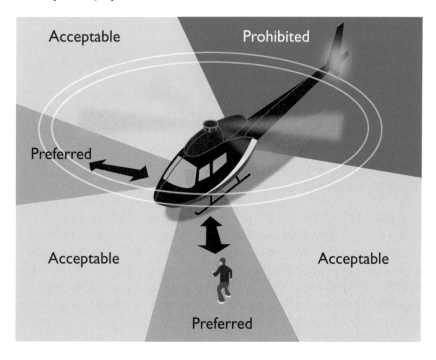

- Never approach a helicopter by walking down a slope, or leave a helicopter by walking up a slope, as you could walk into a rotor blade.
- Helicopter rotors will blow about dust, dirt, sand and loose articles. The landing area must be kept secure, clean and clear of debris.
- When helicopters are taking off or landing, and especially if hovering, the 'down draught' can be tremendous. Be aware of unsecured items being blown up into the rotor or engine air intakes.
- Take extra care when loading or unloading equipment. Keep long or tall items horizontal at waist height, never upright or on your shoulder.
- Once on board, stow all equipment and fasten seat belts.
- The pilot should show you how to exit in an emergency. If you need to disembark while the helicopter is hovering, get out and move away in a slow, controlled manner.

BOAT SAFETY

As a result of global climate changes, greater frequency and severity of flooding and other natural disasters affecting communities in coastal areas has meant that relief operations increasingly require the use of boats. For many aid workers this is an unfamiliar working environment, which presents numerous safety risks. Many of these risks can be mitigated through implementation of safe water practices and the provision of basic safety equipment. The following outlines some simple safety practices for working with boats:

- Make sure the boat is in good condition and has the appropriate certificates for use.
- Watch the weather and plan your trip to ensure you are always one step ahead of a problem.
- Conduct travel by boat in the same manner as vehicle travel – monitor staff movements, ensure that there are regular radio checks, and ensure that you're aware of expected arrival/departure times.
- Make sure that there is suitable safety equipment on board – fire extinguishers, life jackets, communication equipment, flares, spare fuel, first-aid kits, etc.
- Always ensure that every person on board is wearing a life jacket. Make

Relief operations increasingly require the use of boats. For many aid workers this is an unfamiliar working environment, which presents numerous safety risks.

sure that straps, buckles and zippers are in good working order – devices that are ripped or in poor condition should not be used.

- Don't overload the boat with people or equipment. The more weight in a boat, the less responsive it is to sea conditions and to control.
- Don't go beyond the operating limits for the class of the boat. Small boats are not meant for the open ocean.
- Be extremely careful when operating in a shipping channel, as large vessels move at considerable speeds.
- Always keep a proper lookout – especially in late afternoon and early morning when other boats and obstacles can be difficult to see.

7 FIELD COMMUNICATIONS

Good communication systems can be crucial to the success of an organisation's response: they ensure the flow of information within, and to and from, the field. Without them, work will be seriously impaired, or at times impossible. Also, as most humanitarian responses involve a number of different organisations, it's essential that they all have the ability to communicate with each other to facilitate coordination and information exchange. An agency that can't communicate efficiently, both internally and externally, will find it very difficult to adapt to changing situations.

COMMUNICATIONS AND SECURITY

Effective telecommunications are vital for the personal safety and security of staff. It's important to note that satellite phones and radios themselves do not 'create' security: it is the procedures and practices that staff adopt in the field that improve security, while communication equipment is purely an important tool that will enable you to carry out those procedures more effectively.

In insecure environments, it's essential that you always have the means to communicate with other staff, your agency's office, and other organisations. An effective communication system makes it possible to monitor staff movements more effectively, and in the event of potential insecurity it will allow you to alert others, or to be alerted, in order to avoid an incident. Reliable communications also enable you, and other staff members, to call for assistance in the event of a problem – eg, vehicle breakdown or medical emergency – thereby possibly reducing the impact of the incident.

However, in some situations communication equipment and its use can be a source of insecurity. Satellite phones and radios are valuable assets and their prominent use may attract the attention of criminals. Their use can also be regarded with suspicion by local authorities and military groups; in more extreme cases agencies have had equipment confiscated and have been accused of spying. You must be mindful of what information you're communicating and how it may be interpreted by others, and remember that in most situations your communications will be monitored by civil and military authorities, and other groups.

CHOOSING THE RIGHT SYSTEM

Today's global telecommunications environment provides a rich matrix of technologies for use in humanitarian operations. Choosing the appropriate technologies, and balancing factors such as coverage, technical complexity, reliability and costs, presents a major challenge.

When choosing the system, you should consider:
- Your operational requirements – the type of programme, number of staff, spread of project areas and your budget.
- Surrounding terrain – mountainous, low-lying or built-up city area.
- The method of exchange – voice or data.
- The need for a stand-alone system or one integrated with those of other organisations.
- Local regulations and customs restrictions – licensing requirements and the ability to import communication equipment.

The most practical communication options available at present are mobile phones, satellite communications, and VHF and HF radio systems.

In many cases the most appropriate solution is one that combines all the different elements, to ensure the greatest range of options regardless of the physical, technical, legal and political barriers to each system.

In insecure environments, it's essential that you always have the means to communicate with other staff, your agency's office, and other organisations.

Communication equipment

All Save the Children Country Offices must have appropriate communications equipment in all locations that ensure contact is maintained with staff and sub-offices on a day-to-day basis, and must ensure that appropriate back-up systems are in place in case of emergencies.[*]

[*] Save the Children Safety and Security Policy and Standards – Standard 9, February 2010

Save the Children

Mobile phones

In today's relief operations, mobile or cellular phone usage is widespread. Unfortunately, there are still significant problems associated with a communication system that relies solely on mobile phones. In many countries, mobile coverage is limited to cities and major towns, and is often unreliable or non-existent once you travel outside well-populated areas.

In disaster situations, the mobile phone network is unlikely to be working. With widespread power loss, few base stations have the necessary back-up supply to operate. Even if the network survives the disaster, it will very easily become overloaded and you'll have to wait a long time before your call goes through. In areas of armed conflict, mobile phone networks are also likely to be interrupted or turned off by the authorities. Therefore, when working in disaster-affected or insecure areas it's vital to have some form of back-up system in place.

Satellite communication

Satellite systems provide the widest range of options for field communications. Their ability to provide both portable and effective communication links in the most remote locations make them very useful for agencies operating in areas beyond the reach of mobile phones.

Although portable, most satellite systems rely on a direct line-of-sight method of communication. Therefore, antennas must be able to 'see' the satellite. Obstacles such as buildings, trees or hills will reduce their performance. Satellite phones need a clear view to the sky and will work indoors only if fitted with an external antenna, which must be placed outside.

It's important to note that satellite communications can be very expensive to use, especially if you're transferring or receiving large amounts of data, or you're calling another satellite phone or mobile phone. Note also that the satellite signal can be blocked in certain areas at the request of the government – for example, because of military activity or a visit by officials.

There are many different types and providers of satellite communications equipment.

BGAN

The Inmarsat Broadband Global Area Network (BGAN) is a global satellite system that offers both voice and high-speed data communications using portable terminals. The value of BGAN system is that, unlike other satellite data/Internet systems that require bulky satellite dishes to connect, a BGAN terminal is the size of a laptop, making it very portable. However, at around three times the price of the cheaper handheld systems, and with high data costs, the BGAN system is an expensive satellite system to use and tends to be used mainly by humanitarian agencies in emergencies operations or as part of a short-term field visit.

Mini-M

The Inmarsat Mini-M system was for many years the portable satellite system most commonly used by humanitarian agencies. Although they are no longer produced, many agencies continue to use the Mini-M systems in the field. Mini-M phones are compact and mobile, and provide good-quality and relatively cheap international voice communications. However, as data connections are only up to 2.4kbps, data communication and Internet access is not practical.

Handheld satphones

There are now an increasing number of handheld satellite systems available from providers such as Iridium, Thuraya and Inmarsat. While the Iridium phones have almost global coverage, Thuraya phones do not currently cover southern Africa and the Americas, and the Inmarsat handheld satphones only work in Asia, Africa and the Middle East. Although handheld satphones are extremely mobile and relatively cheap, in both hardware and airtime costs, the voice communications quality is not always as reliable as that of the larger satellite systems. However, they do offer a wide range of uses for agencies, particularly where there is a need for discreet mobile communications.

VSAT

One alternative to Inmarsat high-speed data services is the VSAT system. Unlike the Inmarsat's BGAN system, VSAT is not a portable global solution, mainly because of the bulky size of the equipment and the fact that VSAT regional operators in different areas of the world use incompatible equipment. However, VSAT does provide a cost-effective fixed, or limited-mobility, regional solution to accessing broadband Internet and email in remote locations. The VSAT system is an 'always on', fixed-cost service that can provide data speeds ranging from 64kbps to 2Mbps.

Radio communication

The types of radio communication systems commonly used by agencies in field operations are VHF/UHF and HF radio.

VHF (Very High Frequency)/UHF (Ultra High Frequency)

VHF/UHF radios are primarily used for short-range, on-site communications. A typical network of VHF/UHF handheld radios and base unit will allow team members to keep in regular contact with each other and the field base. As VHF/UHF communication is relatively inexpensive and easy to operate, it's very useful for situations that require the frequent sharing of information, such as staff movements and transfer of supplies, etc.

VHF/UHF radio waves travel, mostly, in what are known as 'direct waves'. These propagate in straight lines and provide communication between stations by 'line of sight'. The range of a VHF/UHF network is heavily dependent on the height of the antennas and the topography of the area, but generally the higher your position or your antenna, the longer your range. The typical communication ranges for VHF/UHF radios are:
• Handheld to handheld: up to 2km
• Vehicle unit to vehicle unit: up to 20km
• Base unit to handheld: up to 5km
• Base unit to vehicle unit: up to 20km
• Base unit to base unit: up to 30km.

The distance over which VHF/UHF is effective can be extended with the use of repeater systems. Repeaters receive transmissions from users on one frequency and re-transmit on another, providing greater transmission and reception range; for example, a well-positioned repeater can increase the range of handheld-to-handheld communication to up to 40km. Repeater systems, however, are generally only used in large-scale operations with a number of agencies using the network.

HF (High Frequency)

HF radio is used to communicate over mid- to long-range distances. HF has a much greater range than VHF/UHF because it doesn't require a 'line of sight' between stations. HF equipment is relatively expensive and technical expertise is needed to install the system correctly. Staff will also require training to use it. Since HF units need a lot of power they tend to be quite large and heavy – they aren't very portable. However, HF can be installed in vehicles to provide mobile communications. As well as voice communication, the HF system has the facility for data communication, allowing the transfer of emails and files between remote locations.

HF radio generates two basic types of signals or waves. 'Ground waves' follow the earth's surface for a range of up to 50km and therefore can be affected by the terrain. The second type of HF signal are 'sky waves'. These are transmitted upwards at an angle from the antenna and bounce off the earth's ionosphere back down to the receiving HF radio. This reflection from the ionosphere enables HF signals to reach around the planet's curved surface, in theory for thousands of miles. With HF communication there is a zone between the end of the ground wave and the point where the sky wave returns to earth. This is called the 'skip zone' or 'dead zone' (between 40km and 250km). HF communication within this zone is usually poor. In some situations, variations in the frequencies used and configuration of the antenna can improve reception.

Generally speaking, the higher the frequency you use, the further it will travel. However, the degree at which HF signals are reflected off the ionosphere fluctuates according to the time of day or time of year. You may find some frequencies work perfectly well in the morning, but may be

HF radio signals

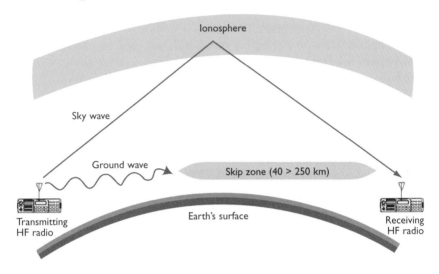

7 FIELD COMMUNICATIONS

unreadable in the evening. In order to maintain good communications at all times of the day, it's important to have a range of frequencies available for use, and to switch between them according to the conditions and the distance over which you need to transmit.

USING A RADIO NETWORK

In some situations, specific protocols and procedures for radio operation may be established, so make sure you're briefed adequately before using the radio. The key point to remember is that radios should only be used for transmitting essential, brief messages regarding your movements, incidents or problems, and other essential operation-related messages, and not for catching up with colleagues and friends.

Call signs are normally used for clarity, in order to clearly identify specific people, organisations, vehicles and places. Quite often, letters of the phonetic alphabet and numbers are adopted as call signs. For example, a programme manager in Save the Children might be called "Sierra One". In cases of an interagency network, your call signs might be issued by the controlling agency.

Speaking on the radio

The radio is equipped with a push-to-talk button that switches the radio from listening mode to transmitting mode. When making a call:
- Make sure that the channel is free and no one is transmitting at the same time.
- Hold the microphone close to your mouth.
- Use standard procedural words.
- Use call signs instead of personal names. Do not identify organisations or personnel by name over the radio.
- When transmitting, speak clearly, not too fast or too slowly, and don't shout.
- Begin by saying the call sign of the station or person you are trying to contact twice; then say "This is", using your own call sign followed by "Over". The receiving station should then answer by repeating your call sign, then "This is" and their call sign, then "Send – Over". Communication between the two stations is now established, and you can start transmitting your message.
- Check the reception quality. Make sure that your message is clearly understood. If in doubt, ask the receiver to repeat the message to confirm.
- Break your message into short sentences, with clear pauses in between.
- Keep communications brief but precise. Stick to the essentials.
- Many radio networks have a designated 'calling channel' and other channels for general transmission. Once you have established contact, move to the appropriate channel.

Misunderstood messages and poor reception can lead to confusion and in some cases an inappropriate response. The use of key procedural words and of the phonetic alphabet to spell out difficult or vital words will help ensure the correct interpretation of messages.

Procedural words

Affirmative/Yes-yes	Yes/correct
Break Break	I wish to interrupt this transmission in order to pass on an urgent message
Copy	Receive
How do you read?	What is my signal strength? Is my transmission clear?
Loud and clear	Your signal and readability are excellent
Negative/No-no	No/incorrect
Nothing heard	I cannot hear you at all
Out	I have finished my transmission. No reply is expected (Over and Out are NEVER used together)
Over	I have finished, your turn to respond
Read back/Repeat	Read back the message as received
Roger	I have understood your last transmission.
Roger so far?	Have you understood this part of my message?
Say again	Repeat your last transmission
Send	Go ahead with your transmission
Spell/I spell	Words require phonetic spelling
Stand-by	I am busy and cannot take your call at the moment
Wait	Wait and I will call you

Phonetic alphabet

A	Alfa
B	Bravo
C	Charlie
D	Delta
E	Echo
F	Foxtrot
G	Golf
H	Hotel
I	India
J	Juliet
K	Kilo
L	Lima
M	Mike
N	November
O	Oscar
P	Papa
Q	Quebec
R	Romeo
S	Sierra
T	Tango
U	Uniform
V	Victor
W	Whisky
X	X-Ray
Y	Yankee
Z	Zulu

7 FIELD COMMUNICATIONS

All staff operating radios must familiarise themselves with emergency call procedures. There may be set procedures established for your radio network, so make sure that you're fully briefed on how to raise an alarm or report an emergency. When communicating an emergency call, usual procedures are to repeat three times "Emergency – Emergency – Emergency" followed by "All Stations" and your call sign, wait for a response then proceed. If you need to interrupt another radio conversation, wait for a pause and call "Break Break" then "This is" and repeat your call sign followed by "I have an emergency, please stand by". Once their communication has finished, proceed with the emergency call.

Any station hearing an emergency call must stop transmitting and listen. All emergency calls must be responded to – ie, you must confirm your receipt of an emergency call and identify yourself. Normal radio communication should not be resumed on that channel until the emergency is over or the station making the emergency call has moved to another channel.

It is important to keep a log of all incoming and outgoing messages. The logbook should record: the time; reception quality; source of the message/transmission; receiving station; key points of the message; and follow-up action points.

Security and confidentiality

Radio communication is not confidential. Be aware that everything you say can be overheard by anyone using a suitable receiver tuned into your frequency. Discussing military movements or sensitive political developments over such a public forum could get you and your organisation into serious difficulties with the authorities or particular groups. Obviously you must be careful about discussing movements of staff, money and supplies over the radio, as this could result in you being targeted by criminal groups. Some agencies use code words and phrases to make sensitive information cryptic. However, staff may struggle to remember confusing codes, and innocent messages may be misinterpreted if a code word is said by accident. Keep it simple.

Power supply

Communication equipment cannot function without adequate power supply. In areas where there is mains power supply, rechargeable batteries with charging kits can be used to provide reliable back-up power. However, in many developing countries the mains power supply is unreliable. The supply can disappear for hours or days without warning and with no information as to when it will come on again. In other situations power supply is simply not available. When planning a communication network it's important to have a separate power back-up system independent of the mains power supply. Options to consider include power inverters, rechargeable batteries, vehicle power supply using cigarette lighter kits, small portable generators, and solar panels.

Radios will only operate if their batteries are charged, so it's critical to keep batteries charged at all times.

It's equally important to ensure that all communication equipment is adequately protected from fluctuations in power supply and power surges. Surge protectors should be issued as standard with all equipment, and all radio bases and antennas must be earthed.

Safety precautions

All radio and satellite equipment can pose a safety hazard, in terms of electrical shock, radio frequency burns or radiation.

You can minimise the electrical hazards by ensuring that all equipment is separately earthed, and cables and plugs are maintained in good order. Cables should be kept as short as possible, and not be placed where they can be snagged by vehicles or people.

Touching a radiating radio antenna or the antenna cable, when they are in use, can cause radio frequency burns. These burns, which appear under the skin, can be very painful and take a long time to heal. Less obvious is the danger from electromagnetic radiation from the satellite antenna's beam. When using a satphone make sure you observe the radiation safety warning and don't position yourself directly in front of the antenna or dish, and warn others in the vicinity.

Maintenance

Expensive communication equipment is easily damaged if it's poorly set up and managed by inexperienced staff. In some locations, broken equipment could have far-reaching implications for staff security. You must ensure the safe and proper set-up and maintenance of all communication equipment. This means placing great emphasis on training and briefing of staff on use of the equipment, and guidelines being made available in the field. In some cases it's worth considering using a technically qualified person to assess and install equipment and carry out training in the field, to ensure that an effective network is established right from the start.

Legal issues

The use of any radio or satellite communication equipment is subject to national and international regulations. In most countries permission must be obtained to operate radios and use certain frequencies. Some countries are also sensitive about satellite communications and ban the use of any satellite equipment in certain areas. In some situations a licence may be required before the equipment can be brought into the country, and this can take a significant time to be processed. However, during a disaster response, some countries waive these requirements. It's important to check with the authorities and other organisations as to what the legal situation is. This could prevent equipment being stuck in customs for weeks.

8 NATURAL HAZARDS AND DISASTERS

In recent years there's been a notable increase in the frequency of natural disasters occurring around the globe. Earthquakes, floods, tsunamis, hurricanes, cyclones, landslides and volcanic eruptions continue to cause colossal loss of life and economic damage every year. While in some countries and regions certain natural hazards are recurring seasonal events and therefore can be planned for, many natural disasters occur with little or no prior warning.

For aid workers, either working in countries or regions prone to natural hazards, or while responding to the aftermath of a natural disaster, these hazards present significant safety concerns. In addition, the confusion, desperation and the breakdown in law and order that often arises in the aftermath of any natural disaster can mean there is a much greater risk of crime and violence.

Although there are specific measures and actions to be taken when dealing with and responding to particular natural hazards such as floods or earthquakes,[*] the most important factor in dealing with any natural disaster is preparedness. Time spent identifying the potential natural hazards in the area where you work, and planning with your colleagues how you should respond before, during and after an event occurs, will pay massive dividends when it comes to minimising the risks to your safety during an unfolding disaster, and can save lives.

[*] The information and guidance provided in this chapter is adapted from the FEMA website (http://www.fema.gov/hazard).

FLOODS

Floods are among the most common, and most destructive, natural hazards. They can be local, affecting a neighbourhood or community, or very large, affecting entire regions. Some floods develop slowly as a result of prolonged rainfall, giving people time to prepare or evacuate. Flash flooding, however, is particularly dangerous, as it forms very quickly and can appear with little or no warning. A flash flood often produces a wall of roaring water that can carry rocks, mud and other debris, and can sweep away most things in its path.

SAVE THE CHILDREN

Working in countries prone to natural hazards, or responding to a natural disaster, presents significant safety concerns.

Minimising the risk

If you know you're in an area that is liable to flood, don't wait until it happens before you react. Prepare for such events by planning with your colleagues what you will do and where to go when a flood happens. If you're working in areas with a high risk of flooding, minimise the risks by following these basic guidelines:

- Know the flood history of your area and find out if a warning system exists.
- When choosing an office or residence, avoid low-lying and flood prone areas.
- Develop an evacuation plan with several alternate routes to high ground.
- Be prepared! Pack a bag with essential items in case you need to evacuate quickly.

What to do during a flood

Most flood-related deaths and injuries occur as a result of people attempting to walk or drive through rising flood water. When flooding starts you should take the following precautions:

If you are on foot:

- Move to higher ground and stay there. Do not walk through flood water, as even shallow water can sweep you off your feet and there may be hidden dangers such as open drains, damaged road surfaces, or submerged debris.
- If you must walk in the water, try to walk where the water is not moving and use a stick to check the firmness of the ground in front of you.

If you are in a vehicle:

- Do not drive into flooded areas. If you come across flood water do not attempt to drive through it, as the water could be much deeper than it appears and you could become stranded or trapped. Turn around and take a different route.

- If you must drive through flood water, drive slowly to prevent the engine from getting wet or the tyres losing their grip.
- Drive with windows open in case a quick escape is necessary.
- If your vehicle loses control or stalls, abandon it and move to higher ground.

If you are in a building:
- If you are in a (solid) multi-storey building, move to one of the higher floors. If possible, move essential items and equipment to an upper floor.
- Switch off the electricity at the main power switch and close the gas valve, but do not touch electrical equipment if you are wet or standing in water.
- Fill bathtubs, sinks and jugs with clean water in case water becomes contaminated.
- If advised to evacuate the area, do so immediately. Evacuation is much simpler and safer before the flood waters become too deep, so leave early enough to avoid being marooned by flooded roads.

What to do after a flood

The dangers associated with floods do not end when the water level recedes; new dangers arise in the aftermath of a flood. Particular care should be taken when re-entering flooded buildings to assess damage or to clean up debris, or while travelling in areas following flooding. It's important to consider the following basic guidance:
- Always ensure the safety of yourself and your colleagues before responding to the needs of others. Do a headcount to make sure all the team members are safe and sound. Check for injuries. Do not attempt to move seriously injured persons unless they're in immediate danger of death or further injury.
- Be aware that additional flooding, flash floods or landslides may occur.
- Stay out of buildings that look badly damaged or if floodwaters remain around the building. Always use extreme caution when entering buildings as there may be structural damage, gas leaks and risks of electrocution from damaged wiring.

- Wear sturdy shoes and use battery-powered lanterns or flashlights when examining buildings. Examine walls, floors, doors and windows to make sure that the building is not in danger of collapsing. Animals, especially snakes, may be hidden inside, so use a stick to poke through any debris.
- Be cautious when driving in areas where flood waters have receded. Roads and bridges may be weakened and could collapse under the weight of a vehicle.
- If landmines and unexploded ordnance (UXOs) are present in the area, be aware that these may have been moved by the flood water.
- Stay away from damaged power lines. Remaining flood water may also be electrically charged from underground or downed power lines.
- Clean and disinfect everything that has become wet. Mud left from floodwater can contain sewage and chemicals. Throw away food that's come in contact with flood waters, and avoid drinking the water supply until you know it's safe to do so.

LANDSLIDES AND DEBRIS FLOWS

Landslides and debris flows (eg, mudslides) can occur in all regions and climates. With a landslide, a mass of rock, earth and debris moves down a slope. Landslides can be large or small, slow or fast, and can happen as a result of an earthquake, storms, volcanic eruption or man-made modifications to the landscape.

Mudslides are basically rivers of rock, mud and earth saturated with water. These are caused by heavy rain and melting snow, which fail to drain properly and cause the earth to become unstable quickly, creating a flowing river of mud or 'slurry'. A mudslide can happen without warning, and move very fast and powerfully, destroying anything in its path, including villages. It can travel several miles from its source, increasing in size and power as it picks up rocks, trees, cars and other materials.

Minimising the risk

If you are working in areas with risk of landslides or debris flows, minimise the dangers by following these basic guidelines:
- Know the risk of landslides or debris flows in your area, and identify which areas or roads are more likely to be affected.
- If there is a significant risk, do not choose an office or residence near steep slopes, close to mountain edges, or near drainage channels or natural erosion valleys.
- Be alert to landslide warning signs such as fences, utility poles, or trees tilting or moving; bulging ground at the base of slopes; any unusual noises such as a faint rumbling sound; trees cracking or boulders knocking together that might indicate moving debris.

What to do during a landslide or debris flow

When a landslide or debris flow occurs you should take the following precautions:
- If indoors, stay inside and take cover under a desk or table.
- If outdoors, move away from the path of a landslide or debris flow as quickly as possible. Run to higher ground or take shelter in a sturdy building or among a group of trees. If escape is not possible, curl into a tight ball and protect your head.
- If in a vehicle, leave the area if possible. If the vehicle stalls or becomes stuck, abandon it immediately and climb to higher ground.

What to do after a landslide or debris flow

Following a landslide or debris flow, consider the following basic guidance:
- Stay away from the slide area. There may be a danger of additional landslides.
- Always ensure the safety of yourself and your colleagues before responding to the needs of others. Do a headcount to make sure all the team members are safe and sound. Check for injuries. Do not attempt to move seriously injured persons unless they're in immediate danger of death or further injury.

- Check for trapped persons near the landslide, without entering the slide area. Direct rescuers to their locations.
- Watch for additional dangers such as damaged electrical, water, gas, and sewage lines.
- If driving in an area affected by a landslide or debris flow, be alert for damaged or weakened roads and bridges.

EARTHQUAKES

Earthquakes strike suddenly, violently, and without warning at any time of the day or night. An earthquake is a sudden shaking of the earth caused by movement along geological fault lines, which can cause buildings and bridges to collapse, resulting in fires, explosions and a high number of deaths. Earthquakes can also trigger tsunamis and landslides. Although earthquakes cannot be predicted, there are geographical areas in which they are more likely to occur.

Global earthquake risk

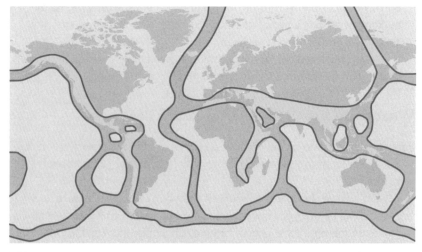

Areas with an increased risk of seismic activity

Although earthquakes cannot be predicted, advance planning can significantly reduce the dangers.

Minimising the risk

Although there are no guarantees of safety during an earthquake, advance planning such as identifying potential hazards can save lives and significantly reduce injuries and property damage. If you are working in areas with a high earthquake risk, reduce the dangers by following these basic guidelines:

- If possible, always choose low-rise buildings that are structurally sound for your office and residence.
- Identify potential hazards that may become damaged or loose or fall during an earthquake. Ensure that gas fittings and electrical wiring is safe and that heavy items are securely fastened to walls. Remember – earthquakes don't kill, but buildings, heavy objects, fires and electrocution do.

- Keep a small 'grab bag' with water and essential supplies (radio, ID card, torch, whistle and some clothing) by the door of your bedroom.
- Fit an earthquake alarm – even a warning of a tremor a few seconds earlier can be enough time for you to get to a place of safety.
- Plan your exit route and identify a prearranged assembly area for all staff. The assembly area should be some distance from surrounding buildings to avoid falling debris.
- Locate safe places in each room – for example, under a sturdy table or desk, in hallways or against an inside wall.
- Know where and how to shut off electricity, gas and water at main switches and valves.
- If possible, securely position emergency supplies, such as water and blankets, outside of your building, so you do not have to re-enter a damaged building to get them.
- Hold earthquake drills with your colleagues and ensure they understand how best to safeguard themselves.

What to do during an earthquake

Be aware that some earthquakes are actually foreshocks and a larger earthquake might still occur. Consider the following basic guidance, according to your position at the time:

If you are in a building:
- **Drop, Cover and Hold On!** Drop to the floor and crawl to a position of cover, such as under a sturdy table or against an inside wall, and hold on.
- Stay away from windows, outside walls, fireplaces and anything that could fall. Protect your head and body with your arms.
- Stay under cover and hold on until the shaking stops, which should be no longer than one minute. If your cover moves, then keep hold and move with it.
- Only ever attempt to exit the building if you are very close to an exit. Most injuries during earthquakes occur because people are hit by falling objects when trying to leave a building. Minimise your movements to a few steps to a nearby safe place, and do not attempt to use stairs, as this is more likely to result in injury.

- Stay inside until the shaking stops and it's safe to go outside.
- If you become trapped in the debris, cover your mouth with a handkerchief or clothing. Do not light a match or use a light switch, in case of gas leaks. Use your whistle or tap on a pipe or wall to help rescuers locate you. Shout only as a last resort – shouting can cause you to inhale dangerous amounts of dust.

If you are outdoors:
- Stay there! Move away from buildings, trees, overhead wires, and poles.
- Clasp hands behind neck, bury face in arms, make body as small as possible, close eyes, and cover ears with forearms.
- Do not move from your position until the shaking stops.

If you are in a vehicle:
- Move to a clear area and avoid buildings, trees, overhanging rocks, bridges, overpasses or utility wires.
- Stop and stay in the vehicle.
- If there is a danger of a structure collapsing on the car, get out and move away.
- Proceed with caution once the shaking has stopped. Avoid bridges and roads that have been damaged by the quake.

What to do after an earthquake

Unexpected and shocking, an earthquake is a terrifying experience for anyone to go through. In the immediate aftermath of any earthquake there will be much confusion, and so consider the following basic guidance:
- Remain calm and move cautiously out of the building – buildings can collapse some time after the quake itself.
- Be prepared for aftershocks. These secondary shock waves are usually less violent than the main quake but can be strong enough to do additional damage to weakened structures. Each time you feel one, Drop, Cover and Hold On!
- Always ensure the safety of yourself and your colleagues before responding to the needs of others. Do a headcount to make sure all the team members are safe and sound. Check for injuries. Do not

attempt to move seriously injured persons unless they're in immediate danger of death or further injury.

- If not there already, move to the pre-arranged assembly area. Watch out for fallen objects, downed electrical wires and weakened walls.
- If it is dark and the electricity goes out, use flashlights or battery-powered lanterns. Do not use candles, matches or open flames indoors after the earthquake, because of possible gas leaks.
- Inspect your building for damage and do not re-enter the building until you know it is safe.
- Look for and extinguish small fires. Turn off the gas and switch off the electricity.
- Check utilities. If you smell gas, hear escaping gas, or see a damaged pipe, then evacuate the building.

TSUNAMIS

Tsunamis are a series of enormous waves created during an earthquake, or another underwater seismic event, that quickly move across the ocean. Although tsunami waves are hardly detectable out at sea, once the waves approach the shore they begin to slow down and gain energy. By the time the first wave strikes, it can be more than 30 metres high and carry immense force. Not all earthquakes will cause a tsunami, but many do. If a major earthquake occurs close to shore, the first in a series of powerful waves could reach the beach within minutes, before a tsunami warning can be issued. Most tsunamis occur in the Pacific Ocean, which is known for its seismic activity, but any coastline can be affected by tsunamis and they can occur far from an earthquake's epicentre.

Minimising the risk

If you are visiting or working in areas at risk from tsunamis, be prepared and minimise the risks by following these basic guidelines:
- Find out about the local tsunami evacuation plans, and whether and how you would be alerted in the event of earthquake.
- If possible, select your office and residence in areas at lowest risk. Know your location's height above sea level and its distance from the coast, as

evacuation orders may be based on these figures. Areas at greater risk are those that are less than eight metres above sea level and within one-and-a-half kilometres of the shoreline.

- Identify a location away from the coastline or as elevated as possible as a meeting point. Tsunami warnings do not give much time for reaction, so make sure you know where to go and the fastest and safest way to get there. Be aware that after an earthquake, roads in and out of an area may be blocked by damage or high volumes of traffic, so always identify more than one route by which to evacuate.
- Prepare a grab bag of essential supplies (food, water, first-aid kit, torch, etc) and store it somewhere easy to locate in an emergency.

What to do during a tsunami

It's possible to survive a tsunami, but you need to know what to do in advance so that you can move quickly if you find yourself at risk. If a tsunami is likely, you should take the following precautions:
- When you know that an earthquake has occurred, listen out for a tsunami warning, if such a system exists.
- If you hear a tsunami warning or detect signs of a tsunami, evacuate at once. Move inland or to higher ground and stay there.
- Do not stay in low-lying coastal areas after a strong earthquake has been felt.
- A noticeable fall in sea level (as the sea retreats away from the shore exposing the seafloor) may precede a tsunami, and you should move away immediately. In some cases a very loud roar, like an oncoming train, may be heard as the tsunami wave rushes toward the shore.
- Never go down to the beach to watch a tsunami come in. If you can see the wave, then you are too close to escape being swept away by it.

What to do after a tsunami

Even though the tsunami has subsided, the remaining debris, destroyed buildings and broken infrastructure still pose a risk to your safety, and therefore you should consider the following basic guidance:

- Always ensure the safety of yourself and your colleagues before responding to the needs of others. Do a headcount to make sure all the team members are safe and sound. Check for injuries. Do not attempt to move seriously injured persons unless they're in immediate danger of death or further injury.
- Stay out of buildings that look badly damaged or if sea water remains around the building. Always use extreme caution when entering buildings, as there may be structural damage, gas leaks and risks of electrocution from damaged wiring.
- Wear sturdy shoes and use battery-powered lanterns or flashlights when examining buildings. Examine walls, floors, doors and windows to make sure that the building is not in danger of collapsing. Animals, especially snakes, may be hidden inside, so use a stick to poke through any debris.
- Be cautious when driving in areas affected by the tsunami, as roads and bridges may have been weakened and could collapse under the weight of a vehicle.
- If landmines and UXOs are present in the area, be aware that these may have been moved by the tsunami.
- Stay away from damaged power lines. Remaining seawater may be electrically charged from underground or downed power lines.
- Clean and disinfect everything that has become wet. Residual mud can contain sewage and chemicals. Throw away food that has come in contact with seawater, and avoid drinking the water supply until you know it's safe to do so.

HURRICANES, TYPHOONS AND CYCLONES

Hurricanes, typhoons and cyclones are regionally specific names for severe tropical storms or tropical cyclones. With winds of more than 100 kilometres per hour moving in a large spiral around a centre of extremely low atmospheric pressure known as the 'eye', tropical cyclones are one of nature's most powerful forces. They can continue for hours or even days, causing widespread damage to buildings and infrastructure, and considerable loss of life. The eye of a tropical cyclone is usually 30 to

Tropical cyclone distribution

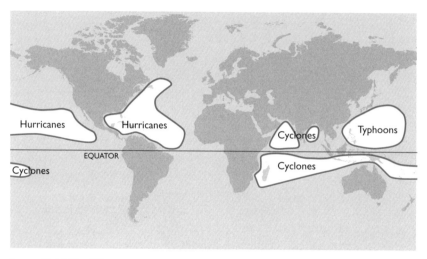

Source: Met Office, UK

50km wide. Around the rim of the eye, or the 'eye wall', winds may gust up to more than 300km/hr. As tropical cyclones near land, they may bring torrential rain, which can result in widespread flash flooding, storm surges and waves that will inundate coastal areas.

Tropical cyclones usually occur at predictable times of year in distinct parts of the world:
- Within the Atlantic/Caribbean region the hurricane season is normally from June to November.
- Within the Pacific/South East Asia region the tropical cyclone season is normally from May to November.
- Within the Far East, South Pacific and Australia region the tropical cyclone and typhoon season is normally from November to April.
- In northern India tropical cyclones usually occur from April to June and September to November.
- The east coast of Africa normally experiences tropical cyclones from November to April.

Minimising the risk

It is difficult to accurately predict where, when and at what strength a tropical cyclone will strike, as they often veer off-course, change their tracking speed and intensify or weaken quite suddenly. If you are in a cyclone region during the tropical cyclone season:

- Make sure that you and all your team members are in a safe location well before the cyclone hits, and make sure the structure is in good condition.
- Be aware of the cyclone warning system that exists in your area.
- Check your house for structural weaknesses and identify a safe room.
- Around the property, secure or remove any loose material that could cause injury and damage during extreme winds.
- In case of a storm surge warning, know the nearest safe high ground and the safest access route to it.
- Have a grab bag ready containing a selection of essential items in case of an emergency evacuation, including an emergency kit (water, food, torch and first-aid kit), warm clothing, waterproof jacket, and personal essentials and valuables in sealable plastic bags.

What to do during a tropical cyclone

If a tropical cyclone is heading your way, you should take the following precautions:

- Once a cyclone warning is issued, secure the doors and board up and tape over the windows to prevent flying glass and other objects from coming in.
- Remain indoors – away from windows, skylights and glass doors – and remain in the strongest part of the building.
- In flood-prone areas do not use the cellar or basement; these areas can be extremely dangerous because of the additional risk of flooding.
- Avoid using naked flames, such as candles and paraffin lamps, as a source of light, in case of gas leaks.
- If the building you are in starts to break up or fall apart, then the only option is to protect yourself with a mattress, rugs, blankets or tarpaulin,

and to hold on to any strong fixtures (such as water pipes), or get under a strong, heavy table or bed.

- Beware the eye of the storm. As the cyclone eye passes over there is a sudden lull in winds, which may last up to two hours. When the other side of the cyclone then hits, winds will resume with equal strength but blowing from the other direction. It is vitally important to remain in shelter during and after the eye passes.
- If you are stuck outdoors during a cyclone, seek solid and enclosed shelter, but avoid trees.
- If you are driving, stop (handbrake on and in gear), park well clear of trees, power lines and streams, and stay in the vehicle.

What to do after a tropical cyclone

Even though the cyclone has moved on or has subsided, damaged buildings, debris and broken infrastructure are a risk to your safety. Consider the following basic guidance:

- If you're in a safe location, stay where you are until officially advised it's safe to leave. If you have evacuated, do not return until authorities say it's safe to return.
- Always ensure the safety of yourself and your colleagues before responding to the needs of others. Do a headcount to make sure all the team members are safe and sound. Check for injuries. Do not attempt to move seriously injured persons unless they're in immediate danger of death or further injury.
- Check for gas leaks. Don't use electric appliances if wet.
- Drive only when necessary. The streets will be filled with debris. Roads may be blocked or weakened. When driving, you be must be careful to avoid damaged power lines, bridges, buildings, trees and any flood waters.
- Stay away from beach fronts, river banks and streams until potential flooding has passed.
- Be cautious when entering a damaged building. Be sure that walls, ceilings and roofs are structurally sound and beware of snakes and vermin that may have been dislodged by the storm.

VOLCANIC ERUPTIONS

Volcanic eruptions happen when lava and gas are discharged from a volcanic vent in the earth's surface. When pressure from gases within the molten rock becomes too great, an eruption occurs, blasting hot solid and molten rock fragments and gases into the air. Sideways-directed volcanic explosions, known as 'lateral blasts', can shoot large pieces of rock at very high speeds for several kilometres. The rock debris from a volcano can crush vehicles and set buildings on fire. The high-risk area around a volcano is about 64km across, but ash can fall hundreds of kilometres downwind.

Volcanic eruptions can also trigger other hazards such as earthquakes, flash floods, landslides and tsunamis. Although it may seem safe to stay at home or in the office and wait out an eruption, doing so could be very dangerous. If you live or work near a known volcano, whether it is active or dormant, be ready to evacuate at a moment's notice.

Minimising the risk

There is usually plenty of warning that a volcano is about to erupt. If you are visiting or working in areas at risk from volcanic activity, be prepared and minimise the risks by following these basic guidelines:

- Find out about the local evacuation plans, and whether and how you would be alerted to a potential eruption.
- Be prepared for additional hazards that can be triggered by volcanic eruptions, such as earthquakes, flash floods, landslides, mudflows, and tsunamis.
- When choosing an office or residence, avoid areas downwind of the volcano if possible.
- Prepare an emergency supplies kit that includes food and water, and goggles and face masks.
- Develop an evacuation plan in case of eruption. Identify in advance where you and your colleagues will meet and where you will go to.

What to do during a volcanic eruption

- Much like a tsunami, a volcano usually requires immediate evacuation to a safer location. Rock debris, lava flows, and ash will make the area around the volcano dangerous to anyone who stays. If an eruption is likely you should take the following precautions:
- If instructed to evacuate, follow the directions of the authorities.
- Evacuate to an area upwind and on higher ground – flash floods, mud and poisonous gases will accumulate in low-lying areas.
- If you are unable to evacuate, seek shelter indoors. Close all windows and doors to keep ash out. Seal up any gaps.
- Store all vehicles and equipment inside a garage and leave them there until the eruption has ended and the dust has settled.
- If you must go outdoors, use goggles to protect your eyes, and use a face mask or hold a damp cloth over your face to aid breathing.
- Avoid falling volcanic ash, cover your mouth and nose, and wear long sleeves to keep your skin covered to avoid irritation or burns. If you wear contact lenses, switch to glasses to reduce eye irritation from ash.
- If you are outdoors and get caught up in a rock fall, roll into a ball to protect your head.
- If you are in a vehicle, keep the engine switched off. Avoid driving when ash is falling heavily, as driving will stir up more ash that may clog your vehicle's engine and cause it to stall.

What to do after a volcanic eruption

Dangers remain after an eruption even if there is no flowing lava. Ongoing tremors, further eruptions and ash fall may make the area uninhabitable for a long time, so consider the following basic guidance:

- Minimise your movements and keep all windows and doors closed.
- Always ensure the safety of yourself and your colleagues before responding to the needs of others. Do a headcount to make sure all the team members are safe and sound. Check for injuries. Do not attempt

to move seriously injured persons unless they're in immediate danger of death or further injury.

- If you must go outside, wear a dust mask and eye goggles.
- Drive slowly and carefully with your lights on – ash is slippery, and stirring it up will clog your engine.
- Remove ash from your roof if you are concerned about its weight. More than ten centimetres of ash may be enough for your roof to collapse.
- Hose down outside with a little water to dampen the ash. This helps to keep it from blowing around.

9 DEALING WITH SECURITY THREATS

Security procedures and guidelines are designed principally to enable you to manage your security and to prevent incidents occurring in the first place. Unfortunately, however rigorously staff follow the guidelines, there are no guarantees that security incidents will not occur. What you should or should not do when faced with a threatening situation is inevitably a judgement you'll make at the time. However, you will react to threats much more effectively the more you are prepared for them.

How you deal with threats will depend on the context in which they arise and the nature of the threat itself. You'll need to respond differently to threats that are deliberately targeted against you or your organisation (eg, armed robbery, kidnapping or death threats) from the way you would to threats arising from being in the wrong place at the wrong time (eg, getting caught up in crossfire or shelling). As a team you must anticipate all likely scenarios and agree in advance how you should respond.

CROSSFIRE AND SHOOTINGS

While aid workers should avoid locations where there is ongoing gunfire, when working in areas of conflict and insecurity the threat of being caught in sudden crossfire is always present. Crossfire is small-arms fire used indiscriminately by any individual or between combatants. Although not directly targeted at you, your very presence puts you at risk of being shot.

Unfortunately, there are no guarantees
that security incidents will not occur.
However, you will react more effectively
the more you are prepared for them.

In some situations, you or your vehicle may be deliberately shot at because of who or what you represent. Although rare, these targeted shootings may be designed to intimidate and harass the humanitarian community, rather than the targeted individual.

Minimising the risk

When operating in an area where there is a risk of crossfire or of being shot at, minimise risk by adhering to the following basic guidance:

- Be alert at all times, particularly around potential targets such as checkpoints and military positions. Keep clear of military convoys: pull aside, let them pass and keep a safe distance from them.

- Enquire about known areas of fighting or previous shootings and, if possible, avoid these areas or any others that are likely to be affected.
- Continually survey your surroundings, and be aware of where you could go for cover if you were fired on.
- Practise with your staff what to do in the event of being suddenly fired on. Routine drills will help staff to react appropriately and immediately.
- Consider improving your site-protection measures, such as window reinforcement and blast walls.

Surviving an incident

The confusion created when suddenly coming under fire can often make it difficult to establish who is shooting, which direction the shooting is coming from, and whether or not you are the target. How you react when shooting occurs will be influenced by your level of awareness at the time, how close you are to the shooting, and what cover is available. Try to keep in mind the following basic guidelines, according to your position at the time.

If you are on foot:
- Seek immediate cover. Drop quickly and lie face down on the ground.
- If you think you are the target, move quickly to a place that is out of sight of your attacker.
- If you assess that the shooting is not aimed at you, lie flat and remain still if it is safe to do so.
- Do not panic or run. Stay calm and try to determine the direction of fire. In built-up areas this will be difficult because of sound echoing off buildings.
- Observe the reaction of the people around you and try to determine what is happening.
- If there is a lull in firing, attempt to improve your cover. Look for a ditch, wall or building nearby. Quickly crawl or move crouched low until you reach cover.
- Decide whether it's possible and safer to move away from the area, or whether to wait for the shooting to cease. Make sure the firing has stopped for some time before leaving your cover.

If you are in a building:
- Keep clear of windows and doors. Resist the urge to look out.
- Do not go out on to balconies or exposed roofs, or into courtyards.
- If the shooting is heavy, lie down. If possible, crawl behind a blast wall or seek protected areas such as a bathroom, basement or under the staircase.
- Wait until the shooting has ceased before leaving your cover to seek information on the situation.

If you are in a vehicle:
- If the road in front of you is clear, drive quickly but safely away from the area.
- If the shooting is in front of you, stop and go back. Reverse slowly to indicate your peaceful intent. Turn around and drive to a safe area.
- If you are coming under direct fire, you will need to stop the vehicle, get out and seek cover away from the vehicle, lying flat on the ground. Crouching behind the vehicle will not protect you.
- Observe the reactions of the people and vehicles around you. Try to determine what is happening.
- If there is a lull in the firing, attempt to improve your cover. Look for a ditch, wall or building nearby. Quickly crawl or move crouched low until you reach cover.
- Make sure the firing has ceased and that it's safe to return to the vehicle before doing so.

SHELLING AND AERIAL BOMBARDMENT

Shelling and aerial bombardment pose a severe threat to everyone in their vicinity. In order to hit a potential target, the attackers often have to saturate a wide area, and if you are within that area you are at risk of being hit.

The array of weapons used can be anything from heavy artillery, rocket launchers and mortars, to fighter planes and helicopters. Mortars have a range of around 6km, heavy artillery up to 25km and rocket launchers up to 50km. Air power has an even greater range. These weapons are utilised because attacks can be launched from long distances, reducing the need for using ground troops, and because they have a deadly effect on the enemy and can be used to terrorise the civilian population.

Although it's rare for humanitarian agencies to be directly targeted by these weapons, there have been many cases where large gatherings of civilians (eg, for food distributions) and humanitarian convoys have been attacked.

Minimising the risk

When operating in an environment where shelling or aerial bombardment may occur, minimise risk by adhering to the following basic guidance:
- Continually gather information from a range of sources on military activity and the tactics and types of weapons likely to be used. Be aware of any military movements in the area.
- Never travel in high-risk areas unless absolutely necessary. Consider informing combatants of your movements and locations to avoid being targeted in error.
- Evaluate the location of your sites. Do not locate your offices, residences or field sites near potential military targets such as airfields, military positions or official buildings.
- Make sure your sites and vehicles are clearly identified and visible from the air. Although this is no guarantee of protection, it may make a pilot think twice before attacking.
- Consider improving your site protection measures such as window reinforcement, blast walls and shelters.
- Be alert at all times. If you hear planes overhead or air raid sirens, or see civilians running for shelter, take evasive action.
- Make sure all staff know how to react and where to seek shelter in the event of shelling or bombing. Practise the drill.

Surviving an incident

If you see or hear shelling or bombing, it will be difficult to ascertain where it's coming from and the intended target, if any. Although you're unlikely to be the target, your particular location may put you at risk. How you react will be influenced by your level of awareness, your proximity to the shelling or bombing, and what cover is available. Try to keep in mind the following basic guidelines, according to your position at the time.

If you are on foot:
- Seek immediate cover. Drop quickly and lie face down on the ground. Shells and mortars explode upwards and outwards, so the lower you are to the ground the greater your chance of not being hit by shrapnel.
- Cover your ears and keep your mouth open to reduce the effect of blast pressure.
- If possible, look for better cover. A ditch or any space below ground level will provide good protection.
- If you hear shelling or bombing, react immediately. This may be only the first round, to be followed by others. It may be that those firing the shells are ranging on to a target by sequentially firing long and short. The initial long shell might be some distance away but the next shell could be dropped very close to you.
- Do not leave your cover until you are sure that the shelling or bombing has stopped.

If you are in a building:
- Seek immediate cover. Move quickly to appropriate shelter, preferably an underground bunker, cellar or emergency trench. If these are not available, move to a safe area on the ground floor, such as in doorways, beneath concrete staircases, etc.
- If you hear shelling or bombing, react immediately. You do not know when or where the next one will land.
- Wait until the shelling or bombing has ceased before leaving your cover to seek information on the situation.

If you are in a vehicle:
- If the shelling or bombing is close by or the vehicle is blocked, stop, get out and run for cover as far from the vehicle as possible. Do not lie near the vehicle as it may explode or create additional shrapnel when hit.
- If the shelling or bombing is some distance away, try to determine the area affected and quickly drive away to safety. If while you are driving

away the shelling or bombing appears closer, stop, leave the vehicle and seek cover.
- Make sure that the shelling or bombing has ceased and that it's safe to return to the vehicle before doing so.

BOMBS AND EXPLOSIONS

In some insecure environments in which aid workers operate, bombs or improvised explosive devices (IEDs) have become an increasingly significant threat. IEDs can come in any shape and form, from letters, to car bombs, and their destructive power is equally varied, from minor injury to major structural damage and mass casualties. The most common type of IEDs are:
- **Roadside IEDs** – usually remotely detonated bombs designed to take out convoys of vehicles.
- **VBIED** – Vehicle-Borne IED or 'car bomb', where a vehicle is packed with explosives to cause massive damage. VBIEDs can come in all shapes and sizes, from a simple passenger car, to a large delivery or sewage truck.
- **BBIED** – Body-Borne IED or 'suicide bomber'.
- **Package-type IED** – letter or parcel bomb designed to kill or maim the person who is opening it.

The level of threat posed by IEDs is dependent, of course, on the type of device used and its intended target. IEDs are usually targeted at specific locations (government buildings, military bases, etc) and high-profile individuals, but in some contexts they are deliberately detonated in public places in order to create mass casualties, widespread destruction and terror. IED attacks can also be highly complex and conducted against multiple targets simultaneously.

Minimising the risk

Despite high-profile bomb attacks against humanitarian organisations in Iraq, Afghanistan and Pakistan for example, it is still rare for humanitarian organisations to be the direct target of a bomb attack. However, in environments where IED incidents occur, there remains a significant risk of getting caught up in these attacks. You should minimise the risks by adhering to the following basic guidance:

- Try to understand the particular nature of the IED threats that exist in your area, where they tend to occur, what type of delivery method is used, who the target is and what the impact has been.
- Identify and avoid high-risk locations such as restaurants, bars, diplomatic areas, or any places that are known to be frequented by people who could be likely targets.
- When travelling, keep your distance from military convoys, or even single military vehicles. Slow down and let them get well ahead of you.

IRIN NEWS (WWW.IRINNEWS.ORG)

In some environments in which aid workers operate, bombs or IEDs have become an increasingly significant threat.

If there is a risk that humanitarian agencies may be the direct target of an IED attack, then you should:

- Be alert, even suspicious, and report the unusual. Bomb attacks are usually well planned, which requires a lengthy period of surveillance of a target. For example, you may notice the same vehicle parked for extended periods of time near a particular location.
- Adopt a low profile and try to vary your routes and routines. Do not travel to and from the office every day by the same route; don't always go to the same restaurants for lunch.
- Strengthen your site security measures, according to the specific threat. For example, a car bomb threat may require you to prevent vehicles from coming within a certain distance of any location regularly used by staff, vehicle searches may need to be conducted by guards, and staff may be required to check their own vehicles for bombs. All of these measures require specialist advice and training.
- Update and rehearse your contingency plans.

Surviving an incident

The chances of your being caught up in an explosion are remote. If you're unlucky enough to be in the vicinity when an explosion occurs, your first response should be to try to reduce the impact of the blast. However, having survived the blast itself, you should also be alert to additional risks that may arise in the immediate aftermath. For example, the initial explosion may be followed by a second bomb meant to cause additional casualties among the police, emergency services and the gathering crowd. Also, following an explosion there will be a great deal of confusion, and the resulting panic and fear may cause people to react aggressively towards those around them; security forces, fearing that they are under attack, may open fire randomly on civilians, or survivors and onlookers may become angry and focus their aggression against you. Therefore, it's important to move away from the area as quickly as possible. Try to keep in mind the following basic guidance, according to your position at the time.

If you are on foot when an explosion occurs:
- Drop instantly to the ground and lie flat, as most blast debris and shrapnel flies upwards from the explosion.
- Wait for the effects of the blast to subside and, if possible, move to better shelter – a ditch, a building or behind a wall.
- Observe the reactions of the people around you to determine what is happening.
- After the explosion, quickly leave the area as soon as you feel it's safe to move.
- Report the incident to your base.

If you are in a vehicle when an explosion occurs:
- If you are able to, or if you feel that you might be the target, drive away as fast as is safely possible.
- If the route is blocked, stop the vehicle, get out quickly and lie flat on the ground, away from the vehicle.
- Once you are at a safe distance, stop and report the incident to your base.

If you are in a building when an explosion occurs:
- Drop to the floor, move away from windows and take cover under a table.
- Wait for the effects of the blast to subside, and if it's safe to do so move into an inner room or a corridor that is better protected than other rooms.
- Stay away from windows and resist the temptation to look out.
- Evacuate the building when it is judged safe to do so or when requested by the authorities.

Responding to a bomb threat

A bomb threat may arise as a result of a telephone call or a written message, or by the discovery of a suspicious package. If you are alerted to a possible bomb threat, it's important to treat it seriously, even if you suspect it might be a hoax. Although very few bomb threats turn out to be real, it is vital that you don't make any assumptions. You must act immediately; there have been cases where slow reactions have resulted in additional deaths and injuries. On discovery of a bomb threat, you must do the following:

- Alert others. Report it immediately to your line manager, activate the fire alarm and tell reception.
- Don't wait for confirmation; evacuate the building and move to a safe distance, which will be hard to judge as it depends on the size of the bomb. For example, it's recommended that you are at least 100 metres away from a small parcel size bomb, 400 metres away from a car bomb and more than one kilometre away from a truck bomb.[*]
- If you find a suspicious-looking item, do not interfere with it; move away and call for specialist assistance. Don't use radios or cellphones in the immediate vicinity of the device. Evacuate all staff to a designated safe area.
- Once out of the building, call the police or appropriate authorities.
- Do not re-enter the building until instructed by your line manager or authorities that all is clear.

LANDMINES AND UXOS

The threats posed by landmines and unexploded ordnance (UXOs) in conflict and post-conflict environments are widespread and extremely dangerous. The social and humanitarian effects of these weapons are far-reaching, as they remain long after the conflict has ceased or the fighting has moved elsewhere.

Mines traditionally have been used as part of a battlefield strategy to defend military positions and key socio-economic targets (eg, water and power supplies). Their principal aim is to delay the enemy's movements, deny them access to certain areas, and in some cases force them through a certain route. Nowadays mines are used more indiscriminately, in ways that leave no record or knowledge of the areas affected. Mines are

[*] BATF Explosive Standards, Bureau of Alcohol, Tobacco, Firearms and Explosives, United States Department of Justice, 2007.

frequently scattered or laid in civilian areas to dislocate communities and disrupt economic activities, targeting agricultural land, water supplies, religious buildings and village paths.

In areas where fighting has occurred there will be various types of unexploded or abandoned military ordnance. Ordnance that either has been fired but failed to detonate, or has been left to deteriorate, is very unstable and could explode at any time.

Types of devices

There is a huge range of lethal devices that can be found in a conflict or post-conflict environment. These devices will vary significantly in form, size, shape and impact.

There are essentially two types of landmine:

- **Anti-personnel mines**. Small in size, these are designed to injure or kill, or put a vehicle out of action. They are detonated by direct pressure or through a tripwire. Anti-personnel mines are categorised as either blast or fragmentation mines. Blast mines are designed to explode when a predetermined pressure (as little as 3kg) is applied to the device. The explosive blast of the mine is what causes injuries or death. Fragmentation mines are detonated when a thin wire or filament is tripped or broken, or when pressure is applied to the mine. On detonation these mines scatter small metal fragments and it is these fragments that cause injuries or death. Most anti-personnel mines are buried in the ground, but the 'bounding' fragmentation mine, once triggered, is thrown up to about waist height and then explodes, sending fragments in all directions. Some other fragmentation mines are directional and are placed above ground, even in trees. Used primarily as an ambush weapon, these are usually set off by a tripwire or fired by hand using a command wire. On detonation, a close pattern of metal fragments is directed at the target.
- **Anti-tank mines**. Larger in size and harbouring more explosive power, anti-tank mines are designed to disable heavy armoured vehicles, but will destroy normal vehicles. Although typically requiring a heavy weight (in excess of 100kg) in order to be activated, over time they can

become unstable and more easily triggered. Anti-tank mines are usually laid underground on main vehicle routes. As they are more easily identified than anti-personnel mines they are often fitted with other devices to prevent them being removed or disarmed.

Other devices include:
- **Unexploded ordnance (UXO)**. This relates to any munitions, ranging from aircraft bombs to bullets, that have been discharged but have not exploded, or have not been discharged but still remain live. Although generally visible, they can be partly or even wholly buried. UXOs can be extremely unstable, particularly over time, and can explode simply when touched.
- **Booby traps**. These are familiar, harmless objects transformed into explosive devices, often to deadly effect. A booby trap can be attached to more or less anything – for example, a door, a toy, a piece of clothing or a well or water pump. When disturbed or used, these everyday items trigger an explosive device.

Minimising the risk

If you are operating in an area where landmines or unexploded ordnance may be present, you should adhere to the following basic guidance:
- Gather information from a wide range of sources (other organisations, authorities, hospitals, etc) on the likely presence of landmines and UXOs in the area.
- Consult the local population on the location of known mines, but take their advice with caution. Misconceptions about the safety or otherwise of specific areas are common. If you are in any doubt, turn back.
- Contact local de-mining organisations, if present, for specific mines awareness information regarding the types of devices you will find in your area of operation, where mines are located, how to identify mined areas, and who to contact should you find yourself or others in a minefield.
- Never travel in high-risk areas unless absolutely necessary. Always avoid old military positions or abandoned buildings: they are almost certain to have been mined.

The threats posed by landmines and unexploded ordnance are far-reaching as they remain long after the conflict has ceased.

- Keep to well-used roads or tracks. Never drive vehicles off a road or track. The military often clear roads and tracks of mines, but rarely the verges, so avoid these as well as lay-bys and other roadside parking places.
- If walking in an unknown area, keep in single file following the same path as the lead person. If practical, maintain at least ten metres between each person, as this would limit casualties in the event of an explosion.
- Local methods of marking known or suspected mined areas will vary from place to place. Familiarise yourself with the official minefield markers used in your locality. They may be warning triangles, signs, painted stones or other less visible markers. Be aware that over time these could have fallen down or become overgrown if not maintained.

- Do not approach, touch or attempt to move any suspicious object. Mines and unexploded ordnance come in all shapes and sizes. If you notice a mine, mark the location clearly and inform the authorities and/or a mine clearance agency.

Recognising mined areas

Mine warfare is based upon the principle of unsuspecting victims activating concealed devices. This of course means that you will not see the mine until it is too late. However, there may be signs or clues as to the presence of mines, which you must stay alert to. Indicators of the presence of mines in an area may include:

- Evidence of previous fighting – eg, battlefield relics such as bunkers, barbed wire, ammunition dumps, helmets, destroyed military vehicles, abandoned weapons, etc.
- Traces of previous explosions, such as small round craters and freshly disturbed ground.
- Animal remains, scraps of footwear or similar signs that something or someone has fallen victim to a mine.
- Abandoned buildings and vehicles, or overgrown and uncultivated fields.
- Out-of-place colours or shapes. Be suspicious of exposed circular rims and metallic or plastic surfaces. But remember that mines can be any shape and made of any material, including wood.
- Bushes, branches or objects that seem out of place.
- Taut, partly buried or tangled thin-gauge wire or filament (similar to fishing line). Never pull on exposed wires.

If you enter a mined area

You are most likely to realise you have entered a mined area when you spot a mine or when one explodes. Whether you are in a vehicle or on foot you must do the following:

- Stop moving. Warn everyone in the vicinity to do likewise. Mines are seldom laid on their own, so assume that others are in the area.
- Assume that you are inside the minefield rather than approaching its edge: who knows how many mines you may have stepped over or driven past to reach your present location?

- Never act impulsively. Mine incidents often cause panic, so calm yourself and your colleagues. Assess the situation carefully before acting.
- If you have radios, call for help. However, be aware that using radios in very close proximity to certain kinds of modern mines can trigger the device to explode.
- Even if you have no means of alerting others, you should stay still and wait for help. Standing still and waiting to be rescued offers the best chance of leaving the minefield safely.
- Only as an *absolute last resort*, when you are positive that no assistance will come, should you attempt to extract yourself from a mined area. In such cases the best option may be to attempt to travel back the way you came, so try to identify the safe ground over which you have travelled. In some cases this may be obvious – a well-used track, for instance – but in others it can be impossible.
- If you are in a vehicle, exit it from the back, either through the rear door or by climbing over the roof. Step only on your vehicle tracks, and walk carefully and slowly in single file, with sufficient space between people, to the last known safe point.
- If you are on foot, try to identify the route you took to your present location. This may be possible in some terrains, but realistically it will be very difficult. Begin to retrace your steps very slowly, examining the ground carefully as you proceed. Warn others behind of any obstacles or route changes. Do not bunch together: move in single file with a safe distance between each person. Do not panic.

If someone is injured by a mine

Dealing with a situation where someone has been injured by a mine is extremely difficult. Often the people are more concerned for the casualty than their own safety. Unfortunately it is common for people to be killed or injured while attempting to rescue people from a minefield. If you are faced with a mine casualty in your vicinity it is vital that you adhere to the following guidance:

- Do not rush to help, even if the person is screaming for help. The initial explosion may have exposed or destabilised other devices, or the victim's body may be concealing untriggered mines.

- Assess the situation before taking any action. Panic and instinctive attempts to help the casualty could result in further injuries and a situation that is even more difficult to bring under control.
- Reassure them. If he or she is conscious, they will be in shock and may try to move or crawl away. Warn them to stay still.
- Assess the casualty's injuries. Do not approach them: base your assessment on what you can see from where you are standing.
- If you have radios, call for assistance. If not, stay still and wait for help if there is a reasonable chance of someone passing by. If you must try and get assistance, identify the last safe ground over which you travelled. Move yourself and other colleagues to a safe area by slowly retracing your steps. Send someone for assistance and wait for it to arrive.
- Only attempt a rescue yourself as an absolute last resort, and even then only if the casualty is alive, needs urgent medical care and no other assistance is available. This must be a common-sense judgement. If you do need to attempt to rescue the casualty, then initially you should try to throw them a rope and drag them out. *Do not* attempt to go in and retrieve them yourself. The desire to help someone in trouble is powerful, but approaching a mine casualty is very risky and may result in you being injured or killed, and the casualty suffering further, and possibly fatal, injuries.

CIVIL DISTURBANCE AND LOOTING

The underlying tensions that exist in many areas where aid agencies operate can lead to civil unrest, mob violence and looting. Actions by local authorities (eg, forced repatriation of refugees) or international events (eg, military action in another country) can cause violent demonstrations to erupt spontaneously. Civil disturbance may be instigated by groups manipulating the situation to further their aims.

Although agencies may not be the focus of the unrest, they may be targeted for their resources by groups who use the chaos and confusion to loot and rob with impunity.

In some cases, aid programmes or the actions of staff members may be the very reason for the unrest. Resentment and frustration over lack of access to essential services may result in staff being attacked and agency assets looted. When international events trigger violent demonstrations, international organisations and their staff may be threatened simply because of who or what they are perceived to represent.

Minimising the risk

In areas with a high risk of civil disturbance and looting, minimise risk by adhering to the following advice:

- Gather information and develop an awareness of the situation. Growing tensions are usually visible well before they erupt into something more serious. Determine who the resentment is aimed at and what events could trigger increasingly violent unrest. Monitor all demonstrations, strikes and public rallies.
- Avoid demonstrations. At times of unrest, limit all staff movements, remain in residences and maintain regular communication with other agencies.
- Reduce visibility if agencies are a potential target. Remove logos from buildings and vehicles.
- If tensions are increasing, consider withdrawing staff who may be at risk because of their ethnicity or nationality.
- Move valuable items from offices and residences to safer locations – for example, move computers, radios and satphones to local staff houses if international agencies are a target.

Surviving an incident

When faced with an angry crowd, there is a natural tendency to try to diffuse the situation. You must be prepared to protect yourself if the scene escalates into violence. How you react will be influenced by your level of awareness, your proximity to the disturbance, and whether the anger is directed at you. Consider the following basic guidelines, according to your position at the time.

If you are on foot:
- Seek information on what is happening.
- Keep your base informed of your location and the situation. Advise them of your next moves.
- Quickly move away from the area of unrest. Seek shelter with another agency, an embassy, local clinic or hospital, or religious building, or with a willing local resident.
- If confronted by an angry crowd, act passive but calm. If possible, and appropriate, identify yourself as a humanitarian worker and try to diffuse the situation. Do not resist any demands.

Resentment and frustration over lack of access to essential services may result in staff being attacked and agency assets looted.

If you are in a building:
- Seek advice from staff and other agencies on what is happening and assess the risks it poses.
- Contact other staff and agencies who might be at risk.
- Ensure that all gates, doors and windows are locked. Instruct guards not to open the gate unless physically threatened.
- If the building is besieged by an angry crowd, think carefully before attempting to diffuse the situation. If the crowd appears violent, consider evacuating the building from another exit. If this is not possible, move to a safe room or shelter.
- If attempting to diffuse the situation, invite a few representatives of the group into the compound to discuss their grievances. Do not go outside the compound. Remember to remain calm, listen attentively, be respectful and avoid making promises. If the crowd appears to become more agitated, leave the area as quickly as possible.
- If you are being looted, do not resist or challenge looters. If possible, try to leave the area in case the situation escalates.

If you are in a vehicle:
- If you see a large crowd ahead of you, stop the vehicle. Carefully reverse, turn around and proceed to a safe location.
- Inform your base of your location and what is happening.
- If your vehicle is confronted by an angry crowd, do not get out. Lock your doors and carefully drive away.
- If the crowd appears agitated and stops your vehicle from leaving, remain calm. If possible, and appropriate, identify yourself as a humanitarian agency and try to diffuse the situation.
- If the crowd becomes violent and you are forced out of your vehicle, do not resist. If necessary, abandon your vehicle and move quickly away from the area.

ARMED ROBBERY

Crime is endemic in many areas where humanitarian agencies operate. Because of the resources agencies possess and the perceived wealth of agency staff, they can often be the target of criminal groups. With the proliferation of weapons in many of these contexts, robberies are frequently armed and in many cases violent. The threats posed by robbery by armed individuals or gangs are often far greater than the threats posed by armed conflict.

Far from being opportunistic, robberies by armed gangs are usually planned well in advance. If during their preliminary reconnaissance the gang members see alert guards, secure gates and an effective perimeter fence, together with good lighting both inside and outside the compound, they will probably look for an easier target.

Minimising the risk

When operating in an environment where armed robbery may occur, minimise risk by following these basic guidelines:

- Seek information. Understand the type of robberies that occur in your area and who the main targets are; whether the assailants are armed or violent; and what the usual outcomes are.
- Limit the amount of cash, valuables and assets stored at your offices and residences. Try to spread the risk by storing these in different places, although it's important to have something to hand over in the event of an armed robbery.
- Be discreet about your financial transactions, especially communications regarding the movement of cash.
- Avoid predictable financial routines that advertise the presence of money. For example, regular visits to the bank to withdraw money, and monthly salary payments that require large amounts of cash to be stored in advance. Use an unmarked vehicle when visiting the bank and try to vary salary payment times to avoid their predictability.
- Make sure you and your colleagues know how to react during an attempted robbery. Everyone, particularly the guards, should be clear about how to deal with armed assailants and how to alert other staff, if this is possible.
- Consider improving site security measures. Establish physical barriers and procedures that will deter or delay break-ins. However, once assailants are inside the perimeter you should limit restrictions so that you do not antagonise them, and ensure that they can leave quickly.

Surviving an incident

All robberies, whether armed or not, are traumatic for the individuals involved. The assailants may be visibly nervous and anxious to make a quick get-away. Armed robberies can pass without any serious risk to staff safety if staff are cooperative and the assailants get what they want. When faced with armed robbery, consider the following basic guidance:

- Remain calm and do not be aggressive. Armed assailants are most likely to shoot when they feel their own safety is threatened.
- Do not attempt to intervene. You will put yourself and your colleagues at risk.
- Comply with demands. No material possessions are worth risking your life for. When faced with demands for a vehicle, equipment or money, do not resist.
- Do not make any sudden movements. Keep your hands visible and inform the armed assailants what you are going to do before you do it.
- If you are held in a group, do not talk among yourselves unless necessary – particularly in a language not understood by your assailants. If necessary, one person should talk on behalf of everyone.
- Once the assailants have left and you feel it's safe to do so, inform the local authorities.

AMBUSH AND ARMED ROBBERY ON THE ROAD

By forcing a vehicle to slow down or stop, assailants can easily ambush a vehicle or convoy to attack or rob it. An ambush can be initiated in a variety of ways: an obstacle placed on the road; a makeshift, unofficial checkpoint; a staged accident or injured person; or concentrated gunfire from a concealed position.

When planning an ambush, attackers will often select areas where they can use the terrain or road conditions to their advantage. This could include: damaged sections of road that force vehicles to travel slowly or bunch together; steep inclines, which limit vehicle manoeuvrability; or sharp 'blind' corners in the road, so drivers will not see the ambush until it is too late.

Minimising the risk

The best defence against vehicle ambush is prior planning to detect and avoid vulnerable areas or times. To minimise risk in areas where ambushes and armed robberies are known to occur, consider the following:

- Seek detailed information on ambushes and armed robberies that occur in your area. Before travelling, consult local people on how to react if your vehicle is shot at or held up. If most vehicles stop when challenged by gunfire, it is usually safest to do the same.
- If possible, vary routes and travel times. Avoid developing patterns.
- Avoid transporting valuable items such as cash through areas where there's a risk of armed robberies. Use discretion when planning such a trip; for example, do not refer to it while using the radio.
- Be alert to abnormal activity along the route. For example, if no one is working in the fields in normally busy areas, there may be a problem.
- If approaching a suspicious area, stop well before it, and if possible let other vehicles pass, and observe them passing through.

Surviving an incident

Being involved in an ambush will create a lot of confusion, which your attackers will exploit. Your reaction should be based on your knowledge of previous incidents and your perception of the attackers' aims. If the ambush is merely to force you to stop so that you can be robbed, then do not take unnecessary risks. If you perceive the ambush has more serious aims and your life is already threatened, you may feel it is necessary to take more evasive action. If you find yourself in an ambush situation, try to keep in mind the following basic guidelines:

- Stop the vehicle when forced to do so. Keep the engine running unless told otherwise.
- Remain calm. Do not become angry or aggressive.
- Keep your hands visible and do not make sudden movements. If you are instructed to get out of the vehicle, do so slowly.
- Always hand over any property demanded by armed assailants. You should not risk your lives to protect property.

- If your vehicle comes under direct fire while you are moving, continue to drive forward at high speed, if possible. Do not attempt to stop and reverse or turn around. It is more difficult to hit a fast-moving target.
- If the driver has been shot or the vehicle immobilised and you are under fire, get out, keeping the vehicle between you and the source of firing. The vehicle will only be useful for concealment and will not protect you from gunfire. Consider moving to better protection such as a ditch, rocks or a building, if possible.

CARJACKING

In many parts of the world stealing vehicles is an attractive source of income. In some cities carjacking has reached epidemic proportions, with armed gangs stealing particular models to order. Humanitarian agencies have been particularly targeted by carjackers, because of the types of vehicles they use. Carjacking can occur anywhere but is most common at traffic lights, road intersections, fuel stations, or outside an agency's office or residence. Carjackers may deliberately stage an accident to induce the driver to stop and get out of their vehicle. Carjacking is potentially very dangerous, as often the carjackers are armed and nervous, and will resort to violence quickly in order to steal the vehicle.

Minimising the risk

When operating in areas with a significant risk of carjacking, the following guidelines should enable you to minimise risk:
- Gather information on carjacking incidents in your area, including the types of vehicles targeted and the techniques used; the specific locations affected and at what time of day; and the level of violence used. Try to identify patterns and adapt your security procedures appropriately. If a particular type of vehicle is being targeted, think about using a different model.
- Avoid areas where carjacking is known to occur. If possible, avoid 'choke points' such as traffic lights and narrow streets, where you may be especially vulnerable.

Carjacking is potentially very dangerous, as often the carjackers are armed and nervous, and will resort to violence quickly in order to steal the vehicle.

- Avoid stopping outside your residence while the gates are being opened. Arrange a signal with the guards or staff so they can open the gates in time for you to drive straight in without waiting.
- Carjacking often takes place after dark, so avoid travel during the evening.
- Vary routes and travel times. Avoid developing patterns.
- Consider travelling with another vehicle or in convoy, as carjackers rarely wish to confront more than one vehicle.
- Keep doors locked and windows closed, particularly when driving through crowded areas.
- Make sure all staff, particularly drivers, know how to react when dealing with an attempted carjacking.

Surviving an incident

Being confronted by an armed carjacker is both dangerous and traumatic. Remember, it is only the vehicle they are after: enabling them to take it without any interference is the safest way to handle an incident. When faced with a carjacking incident you should try to do the following:

- Stop the vehicle. Apply the handbrake, but keep the engine running in neutral.
- Get out only when instructed to do so. If you have to exit the vehicle, leave the door open with the key in the ignition.
- Keep your hands visible and do not make any sudden movements. Be especially careful when reaching to release your seatbelt. When complying with demands, move slowly and tell the assailant what you intend to do prior to doing it.
- Remain calm. Do not become aggressive or try to negotiate.
- Be compliant to demands. Do not risk your life for a vehicle, and surrender personal valuables if demanded.
- If in a group, do not talk among yourselves more than is necessary, particularly in a language not understood by your assailants.
- Allow the carjackers to depart without interference.
- Report the incident to the local authorities.

BRIBERY AND EXTORTION

Aid workers are at times drawn into situations involving bribes or extortion. For example, you may be asked to pay an incentive to ensure that official documents are processed quickly, or you may be 'encouraged' to buy your way out of a difficult situation such as an alleged traffic offence. Bribery or demands for 'gifts' at road blocks or checkpoints is a common problem that you may have to deal with. Complying with these requests not only affects the credibility of your organisation, it may create a precedent that results in increasing demands being made in the future. In more extreme situations, staff members or organisations may be threatened with violence or reprisals – for example, if they do not pay armed gangs part of their salary or some form of protection money.

Definitions

It's important to understand the difference between bribery and extortion, as this will help you determine how to respond. Key definitions are:

- **Bribery** – is the provision of money, gifts or favours to persuade someone to act dishonestly or to unduly influence a decision. Bribery is a crime in many countries and is also in breach of most organisations' staff behavioural codes.
- **Extortion** – is a form of blackmail where threats are issued against an individual unless demands – usually for payment – are met. Sometimes such threats may involve threats of physical harm.

Dealing with demands

How you respond to demands for money or gifts will depend on the circumstances and the degree of threat to your safety. If the demands are associated with threats of violence, then it's important to report the incident to your line manager. While every situation is different, if requests or demands are made of you, it's important to adhere to the following basic principles:

- Politely refuse to pay.
- If they persist with a request/demands for payment, inform them that your organisation prohibits payment of bribes, and even draw their attention to the staff code of conduct.
- If the situation is not resolved, ask to see a more senior official or manager.
- If unsuccessful, leave and report the incident to your line manager.
- If your personal safety or that of your colleagues would be endangered by a refusal to pay, then pay the bribe and report the incident to your line manager.

ARREST AND DETENTION

Unfortunately, many international and national staff working with humanitarian organisations have been detained or arrested while carrying out their work. In some cases, aid workers have been detained in police stations or other government premises for hours or even days, accused of lacking the correct travel permits or visa documentation. Aid workers have also been detained and arrested for 'suspicious activity'; for example, writing reports or posting web blog entries that the government perceived as critical of the country's political or human rights situation. While the underlying cause of many of these detentions or arrests is related to the work and activities of the staff members' organisation, in some instances the individual arrested will have committed an offence or can be reasonably suspected of having done so.

In other situations, aid workers have been detained by local communities or beneficiaries and not permitted to freely leave a village or camp. Often this was a result of disputes or frustrations with the agency's programme activities or a distribution process.

Definitions

It's important to understand the specific type of threat you are facing, as this will enable you to determine the most appropriate response. Key definitions are:

- **Arrest** – the detention and seizure of a person, whether or not by physical force, by someone acting under authority (police or military) in connection with a crime or offence or infraction and where the person is not free to leave.
- **Detention** – a person or group is held against their will by an individual or group (eg, villagers, local authority or military). While there is no intention to cause harm, there is also no clear precondition for their release. Reasons for detention can range from unhappiness with an agency or its programmes, to concerns for the 'security' of the staff.

Minimising the risks

When operating in an area where there's a risk of being detained or arrested, minimise the risk by adhering to the following basic guidance:

- Develop good relations with local authorities, security actors and the community.
- Maintain appropriate behaviour, both on and off duty.
- Know and comply with key local laws and customs.
- Ensure that all legal documentation (visas, travel permits, radio licences, etc) are up to date.
- Do not carry any politically sensitive documents or reports, especially through customs.
- Be conscious of the information you convey in emails or reports, or discuss over the phone.

Responding to an arrest

If you should find yourself arrested or detained by the police or military, the following basic advice will help you to respond to the situation – even though its relevance will vary according to the specific context:
- Do not resist; this will only weaken your case.
- Cooperate fully with the authorities that have detained or arrested you.
- Remain calm and avoid showing any signs of anger or hostility.
- If you are with other colleagues, try to stay together. Consider appointing one spokesperson among you.
- Try to determine why you've been detained or arrested and what evidence they have against you.
- Ask permission to phone your office or ask them to contact the office on your behalf.
- If possible, keep your passport with you and use your ID card as identification.
- Remember that your organisation will be doing everything within its capacity to secure your release.

Negotiating release from detention

If you find yourself being detained, whether by local villagers, armed groups at a checkpoint, or the local authority, the main issue will be your ability to carefully negotiate your release. As the build-up to, and reasons for, your detention can vary significantly, there are no set guidelines for securing your release, but the following key principles will help you deal with the situation:*

- Remain calm and cooperative. Do not antagonise those detaining you by issuing demands to be released.
- Listen carefully to those detaining you, to try to establish what they want and why.
- Your negotiations should focus on gaining permission for you to leave freely, rather than on dealing with the concerns or demands of those detaining you.
- Don't make promises you can't deliver in order to be released quickly. Listen to the requests of those detaining you, make it clear you're taking note of their concerns and will follow them up. Indicate that you're not in a position to make final decisions and would need to consult with your colleagues or headquarters.
- If you remain detained, or you can't negotiate a way out, make it clear that you have no authority to make decisions and that you must be allowed to communicate their concerns with your field base or headquarters. Keep negotiating for this, as it's vital that you establish contact with your agency.

ABDUCTION, KIDNAPPING AND HOSTAGE SITUATIONS

Although it's rare for humanitarian aid workers to be abducted, taken hostage or kidnapped for ransom, in recent years there has been a growing number of incidents around the world.[†]

National and international aid workers have been taken hostage in an attempt to add weight to political or ideological demands, or in order to secure the release of political prisoners, or to draw media attention to a localised dispute. However, increasingly, aid workers have become the targets of criminal gangs seeking to obtain a ransom. Nowadays kidnapping is big

> ## No ransom policy
>
> Save the Children will not pay any ransom to effect the release of a member of staff. However, Save the Children will use all appropriate means to secure their release.[*]
>
> In the event of a member of staff being abducted, a Crisis Management Team (CMT) will be established at Head Office and the respective Save the Children CEO will assume ultimate decision-making authority. The CMT will liaise with staff in the field and coordinate all activities.
>
> [*] Save the Children Safety and Security Policy and Standards – Standard 13, February 2010
>
>  **Save the Children**

business and many abductions are motivated by profit rather than principle. Economic kidnapping is one of the fastest-growing criminal industries, estimated to be worth $500 million each year.[*] Kidnapping for ransom continues to be common in Colombia, Mexico, Brazil, Honduras, Venezuela, India, Indonesia, Philippines, Russia, Somalia, Kenya and Nigeria, among others.

It's important to bear in mind that the motivations of captors may change over time. What may have started out as a politically inspired hostage situation may become a kidnapping incident as captors seek a ransom when initial demands fail.

Definitions

Understanding the type of threat you are facing will enable you to determine how best to minimise the risk and what to expect in terms of possible motives, conditions and treatment, and your overall chances of survival. Key definitions are:

[*] R Briggs, *The Kidnapping Business*, The Foreign Policy Centre, London, 2001.

9 DEALING WITH SECURITY THREATS

- **Abduction**: a person or group is forcibly taken against their will, but no demands are made. Abductors intend to cause harm or force the abductees to do something for their benefit. Kidnapping and hostage situations are considered as abductions until demands are made.
- **Kidnapping**: a person or group is taken and then threatened with harm in order that money, goods or services can be extorted from either the individuals or those associated with them (eg, friends, relatives or employers), in exchange for their safe release.
- **Hostage**: a person or group is held with their safety and subsequent release dependent on the fulfilment of certain conditions. These conditions may include: the publicising of a political cause; the exchange of hostages for political prisoners; or the evasion of prosecution by criminals when their activity has been discovered by the authorities.

In many cases it will be difficult to determine whether an incident is an abduction, kidnapping or hostage situation until any demands are made or credible information is received. Kidnapping demands may not be issued for some time – in some cases days, weeks or even months after the event.

Minimising the risk

When operating in an area where the risk of abduction, kidnapping or hostage-taking is present, minimise the risk by adhering to the following basic guidance:

- Understand the threat. Be aware of the types of incidents that have occurred in the past, and the main targets and perpetrators; how and where incidents normally occur; and how abductions and kidnappings are traditionally dealt with by the local community.
- Be familiar with the local security procedures. Discuss within your team appropriate responses to an abduction attempt. It's important that everyone is aware of how best to behave in the event of an incident.
- Be prepared. In a high-risk environment it is important, at all times, to be dressed appropriately and carry items you may need in the event of an abduction, such as medication and emergency contact details.

- Avoid routine. Kidnapping in particular requires planning, and so perpetrators will study their target's activities and movements for some time before attempting the abduction.
- Maintain a low profile. Consider removing agency logos from vehicles and property, travelling in unmarked local vehicles, and even withdrawing those staff members considered to be at highest risk.
- Avoid travelling alone, especially at night. Perpetrators may be less likely to attempt to abduct people travelling in groups, as this requires more planning and resources.

(IRIN NEWS (WWW.IRINNEWS.ORG)

Although it's rare for aid workers to be abducted, in recent years there has been a growing number of incidents around the world.

- Always keep your office informed of your movements. They should always be aware of where you are travelling to and when you are due to arrive.
- Report any suspicious activity. Most abductions are planned and the victims are often observed for some time before being captured. Always report suspicious activity to your security focal point or manager.

Dealing with an abduction

The most dangerous moments are often when you are initially taken or when you are being moved by your captors. This is when your captors are taking the most risks and may be nervous and therefore more prone to violence. For victims, the confusion and fear of not knowing what will happen next is possibly the most difficult thing to deal with, particularly in the early stages. The following will help enhance your ability to cope with the situation:

- Remain calm. It is important to stay as calm and composed as possible to avoid increasing the already heightened tension of the situation. Do nothing to excite or upset your captors.
- Do not resist. In many cases overwhelming force will be used to capture you, and therefore any attempt to avoid capture or escape could result in death or injury to yourself or your colleagues. If you are in a group, try to stay together.
- During your capture you may be blindfolded, restrained, beaten and even drugged. Do not resist this, as the main purpose is to keep you quiet.
- Use all your senses to establish what is happening. Start to build a picture of what is happening to you and memorise as much as you can. How many people abducted you? Are you being moved in a car? How long are you travelling for? Can you identify your surroundings? When you are released these details may help the authorities to free other victims.

While in captivity

Once in captivity there is generally very little you can do to influence the situation, as negotiations will usually occur between your captors, the host government, your agency and in some cases your home government. However, there are strategies that you can employ to increase your chances of survival. It is important that you:

- Accept that you are in a very dangerous situation and prepare for a long and tough experience. Remember that your chances of being released alive and unharmed are excellent, but it is important to be physically, mentally and emotionally prepared for a difficult experience.
- Try to keep your personal belongings, clothes and identification. Unless forced to hand them over, try to avoid accepting an exchange of clothes as this could put you at risk during a rescue attempt.
- Expect rough treatment. Your abductors will often threaten you or try to demoralise and humiliate you; it makes you easier to control and manage. Bear in mind that you have a value and ultimately your captors will want to keep you alive and well.
- Be sceptical of information given by your captors, as they may often make false promises of imminent release.
- Try to establish a rapport with your captors, if it feels safe. Attempt to show yourself as a real person rather than a commodity. Family is a universal subject, as are sports and many hobbies. Listen actively to their feelings and concerns, but never debate their cause.
- *Do not try to escape.* You risk being killed by a nervous captor and, if you were part of a group who were taken, you could jeopardise the security of those left behind.
- Try to stay healthy and maintain your strength. Eat the food you are given and drink plenty of water. Try to stay clean and exercise as much as you can. Once a level of rapport or communication is achieved, try asking for items that will increase your personal comfort. Don't be afraid to ask for washing and toilet facilities, medicines, books or papers.
- Be patient, as negotiations will be difficult and time-consuming, and during these you may be held in the same place or moved several times. Remember that your chances of survival increase with time.

- Above all, remember that *your one and only goal is to survive*. Remain confident that your organisation is doing all it can to secure your release and at the same time is supporting your family and friends. Keep this in mind even if you are not aware of any progress, or if your captors tell you differently.

During your release

Your release may be as tense and dangerous as your initial capture. In most cases the release follows lengthy negotiations, and the situation will be confusing and subject to constant changes. It's likely that your captors will be nervous and fearful of capture. When the time comes for release, you should proceed with great care, and it is important that you:

- Listen to orders given by your captors and obey them immediately.
- Do not make sudden or unexpected moves.
- Stay alert. Be prepared to act quickly if things go wrong.
- Be prepared for delays and disappointments.

Surviving a rescue attempt

It is also important to prepare yourself mentally for what will happen if the authorities carry out a rescue attempt. During a rescue there will probably be a series of deafening and blinding explosions, clouds of tear gas and total confusion. If you are mentally prepared for this, you stand a better chance of escaping unharmed. You should try to follow these guidelines:

- Do not run. Drop to the floor and seek cover. Keep your hands on your head.
- Wait where you are until discovered.
- Do not make any sudden or unexpected moves.
- Immediately follow any instructions given by the rescue team.
- Try to identify yourself, but be prepared to be handled roughly by the rescue team: until you are formally identified they will treat everyone as a potential captor.

DEATH THREATS

Death threats or threats of violence issued to staff by individuals or groups must be taken seriously. Threats to agency staff are common in many countries. While the majority of these threats are empty or unfulfilled, many others have developed into serious security situations.

Threats can be politically, ethnically, religiously or personally motivated. They may be targeted against an individual staff member (eg, because of their behaviour such as entering into a controversial relationship), an organisation (eg, by an ex-employee disgruntled by their dismissal) or the humanitarian community as a whole (eg, to deter their presence in a particular area or country).

Threats can be received in a number of ways: a staff member may be threatened in person; threats may be issued by letter, email or telephone or by delivering a symbolic object such as a bullet; or leaflets containing the threat may be distributed throughout a community.

Dealing with a death threat

If you or a colleague experience any threat, it is imperative that action is taken immediately. You should follow these guidelines:
* Document the incident. Write down exactly what was said or done by the perpetrator and if possible provide a description. Do this as soon as possible after the incident, while it is fresh in your mind.
* Report the incident to your manager and/or your organisation's headquarters.
* Immediately report the threat to the appropriate local authorities, and make sure it is investigated thoroughly.
* If after your investigations you believe the threat to be a real risk, review your current security measures. If a staff member is threatened, you may consider temporarily relocating them while the situation is dealt with, although their removal may be the intended aim of the threat.
* Be aware that empty threats against an individual or organisation can be just as distressing as the real thing, and should also be thoroughly investigated.

SEXUAL VIOLENCE AND ASSAULT

Sexual violence is a threat in any society, and all age, ethnic and economic groups are at risk. The vast majority of sexual assaults are committed by men against women, but attacks on men do occur. Perpetrators may target victims known to them or will select them opportunely – for example, when carrying out another crime. In conflict environments where many aid agencies operate, the sexual violence risks are significantly heightened. There have been numerous incidents where aid agency staff have been subjected to violent assault by groups or individuals.

There may be various motives for the use of sexual violence against aid agency staff. It may be a politically motivated act to intimidate an agency or the aid community. It could be that the perpetrator harbours feelings of hatred and frustration towards an agency or another individual in that agency, rather than towards the victim.

Minimising the risk

The risk of sexual violence will be present in all programme locations. To minimise this risk you should adhere to the following basic guidance:
- Be aware of potential threats by researching the types of incidents that have occurred in the past, who has been targeted and who the perpetrators were.
- You may need to review your security measures and procedures, making sure that staff are not exposed through movement procedures, accommodation arrangements, or their working environment.
- In high-risk situations you may have to consider the need to relocate or withdraw those staff at highest risk.

Surviving an incident

There is no effective guidance on what to do when faced with sexual violence and assault. Your reactions will be based on the number of attackers, who they are and whether they are armed; where the attack occurs; whether there may be help close by; and your own personal capabilities. Victims may react with one or a combination of the following:*

- **Passive resistance**: doing or saying anything that will persuade or intimidate an attacker into changing their mind.
- **Active resistance**: using anger and physical force to distract or fight off the attacker, including struggling, screaming or running away. This could lead to an increased violent response.
- **No resistance**: by doing nothing, attempting to preserve life and minimise the physical harm that is done during the assault.

If you are forced to witness a sexual assault, do not attempt to intervene if you could be seriously injured or killed. As well as being unable to help the victim, you may provoke the attacker into further violence against them.

After the assault

There are no 'correct' ways to deal with the aftermath of a sexual assault. Everyone copes with trauma and shock in their own way. If you have been subjected to a sexual assault, consider the following:

- Talk to someone you trust. Although you may think you are coping, it's important to get emotional support as quickly as possible after the event.
- You must inform your organisation, as they can offer appropriate medical and professional support.
- You may have suffered physical injury as a result of the assault. Seek medical treatment and make sure someone accompanies you to the hospital to provide support during your treatment.
- It may be advisable for you to take post-exposure prophylaxis (PEP) to reduce the risks of HIV infection. It's important that you seek medical advice quickly to determine your level of exposure and to discuss the benefits and risks of PEP treatment. Although it does not guarantee protection from HIV infection, if you start using PEP within one or two hours of an incident, it may significantly reduce the risk of developing HIV. Starting PEP within 48 or even 72 hours may still offer some protection, but the greatest protective value is in starting it immediately.

* Adapted from *Be Safe Be Secure: Security Guidelines for Women*, UNDSS, New York, 2006.

Post-exposure prophylaxis (PEP) guidance

All Save the Children Country Offices should provide staff with clear information and guidelines on how and where to obtain post-exposure prophylaxis (PEP) quickly (ideally within a few hours, and no later than 72 hours post-exposure) in cases of rape, needle stick injuries, or other potential exposure to HIV. Where necessary, arrangements should be made in advance with a suitable medical practitioner or other organisations. If staff members are travelling, or working in areas where PEP is not available then 'PEP kits' should be supplied. All staff should seek medical advice before taking PEP, including when and how to use the treatment, and the possible side effects.

Further information on PEP and additional support can be found in Save the Children's Post-exposure Prophylaxis Guidelines.

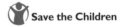 **Save the Children**

- You must decide whether you want to report the crime to the authorities. If you do report the crime to the police, they will probably recommend or insist on a hospital examination. The medical examination may include a test for sexually transmitted diseases.
- In most cases, the police will conduct an investigation that will include you being questioned about the circumstances of the event.
- Although it's important to take time off to recover, you may want to remain in your current location where you have support from colleagues and friends. Ultimately the decision should be yours, but it may be helpful to discuss the options with your colleagues and organisation.
- No matter how long after the event, professional support will be available and encouraged through your organisation.

10 RELOCATING AND EVACUATING STAFF

For agencies working in insecure environments there is always the risk that the security situation will deteriorate to such an extent that it's no longer safe, or acceptable, for staff to remain. As a result, it may be necessary for staff to relocate to a safer site within the country. In more extreme situations, staff may have to be evacuated to the safety of a neighbouring or nearby country. Relocation or evacuation may not always be an option, however; it may be too dangerous or for some other reason not possible for staff to withdraw. In these situations staff may have to stay put and wait for the situation to calm.

The need to relocate or evacuate staff often arises in an atmosphere of crisis and chaos; preparedness is crucial to enable you to respond effectively to changes in the security situation. Agencies operating in insecure locations must develop contingency plans for a possible deterioration in security, and must have in place a range of options available to facilitate the safe and efficient evacuation or relocation of staff.

DEFINITIONS

Although different agencies may use different terminology when referring to the withdrawal of staff, the following terms are defined here to ensure common understanding.

- **Suspension**: the temporary curtailment of programme activities either to avoid emerging threats or, following an incident, to allow time for reflection on the security situation.

- **Relocation**: the physical withdrawal of staff (and assets) from the crisis area to a safer location within the same country.
- **Evacuation**: the physical withdrawal of staff (and assets) from the crisis area across an international border.
- **Hibernation**: staff remaining in one or more locations, or moving to a pre-arranged meeting point, during a crisis because relocation or evacuation is not possible or is too dangerous, or the agency chooses to remain.

Suspension of programme activities and/or the withdrawal of staff is seen as the ultimate, and often most difficult, action an agency can take

Agencies operating in insecure locations must develop contingency plans for the safe evacuation or relocation of staff.

in response to security threats. It may be initiated in advance of possible insecurity, to avoid staff being exposed to threats, or as an emergency response to a sudden deterioration in security.

A planned relocation or evacuation should allow sufficient time to organise the withdrawal of staff and to secure or remove assets and important documents. Withdrawal may involve the partial relocation or evacuation of non-essential staff, leaving behind a core staff to continue essential activities or maintain an official presence. Alternatively, withdrawal could involve the complete relocation or evacuation of all staff, ceasing all activities, and leaving behind no official presence.

When relocation or evacuation occurs in direct response to a sudden and unforeseen deterioration in the security situation that makes staff presence untenable, the priority is to move staff away from the area as quickly as possible. An agency may withdraw on its own or as part of a wider inter-agency evacuation coordinated by another international organisation – for example, the UN. The method of withdrawal will be dictated by the availability of transport in the field site, the timing of evacuation or relocation (day or night), and the location of the threat.

WHEN TO WITHDRAW

Agencies will relocate or evacuate staff from a location to ensure they are not exposed to unnecessary risks. Ideally this decision will be taken before staff are put in danger, but situations can deteriorate rapidly, forcing staff to flee for safety. Circumstances where relocation or evacuation of staff becomes necessary may include one, or a number, of the following:

- Staff are exposed to unreasonable risk.
- Humanitarian agencies are being targeted.
- There is an immediate threat – eg, fighting in the vicinity.
- Security concerns make it impossible to meet programme outputs and the needs of beneficiaries.
- Controlling forces/authorities recommend departure.
- Embassies/UN officials advise foreign nationals to leave.

Determining when to evacuate or relocate can be complicated by agencies having different interpretations of the security situation, or being more or less willing to accept higher levels of risk because of their mandates. Consequently, some agencies may choose to withdraw staff before or after other agencies.

The relocation or evacuation of humanitarian agencies can aggravate the security situation, as it may indicate to the local population that the situation is dangerous. It could also be seen as a removal of the safety barrier that the humanitarian community's presence may have symbolised. The withdrawal of staff is a highly public act, which has a great bearing on an agency's image within a community or country. If it is not handled correctly it can be very difficult to restore relations with authorities, beneficiaries and the local community when you return.

The decision to relocate or evacuate is never easy; it can be difficult for staff to abandon colleagues and friends, and months of work. Some staff will want to remain or will feel that their agency is overreacting or acting too cautiously. Regardless of this, the ultimate decision will be taken by your agency's headquarters. However, the withdrawal will be more efficient if this decision is taken in consultation with field staff.

DEVELOPING RELOCATION/EVACUATION PLANS

Agencies operating where there is a risk of evacuation or relocation becoming necessary must draw up contingency plans as part of their local safety and security plans. These should outline all possible scenarios, including emergency relocation or evacuation, partial or complete withdrawal, or the hibernation of staff. Plans must provide detailed guidance on the procedures and measures that staff should undertake.

It's important that all staff are involved in the process of developing contingency plans. This will ensure that they understand the issues and will be more likely to 'buy into' and adhere to the plan. Planning as a

Contingency planning

All Save the Children Country Office Safety and Security Management Plans (SSMPs) must include contingency plans that address the possible relocation and evacuation of staff, and the suspension of operations. These plans must be reviewed and updated on a regular basis.[*]

[*] Save the Children Safety and Security Policy and Standards – Standard 2, February 2010

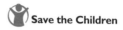 **Save the Children**

team will help identify the essential information and resources needed, and the range of tasks involved, to ensure the safe and efficient withdrawal of staff.

Regardless of whether your agency participates in an inter-agency or UN evacuation plan, it must also prepare an independent plan. This is vital in case there are problems with the joint evacuation or if your agency chooses to leave before the inter-agency evacuation is initiated.

The plan must clearly indicate your agency's responsibility to both national and international staff in the event of a relocation or evacuation. National staff may be split into two groups: those who originate from the area, and those who have been relocated from elsewhere in the country to work in the area. While most agencies will endeavour to return national staff to their homes, or a safe location in-country, it is rare for agencies to evacuate national staff across international borders. Where national staff cannot be incorporated into the relocation or evacuation plan, an agency should work with its staff to identify what support and resources it could contribute to ensure that staff can relocate themselves, if they wish, to a safer area in-country.

Contingency plans should also detail the arrangements for certain staff to assume responsibility for offices and programmes, in the event of senior

Staff evacuation/relocation policy*

In the event of extreme threat or a significant deterioration in security, Save the Children will evacuate international staff and accompanying dependants to a safe place in a neighbouring country or to their country of domicile.

Save the Children will not evacuate national staff or their families except in the most extreme circumstances.

Save the Children will endeavour to relocate national staff and their immediate families who were posted elsewhere in the country by Save the Children to a safer place within the country.

Save the Children will endeavour to assist in the relocation of any national staff and their immediate families who are at risk directly as a consequence of their work with Save the Children, or because of their ethnic origin, or if they are exposed to an imminent or targeted threat. However, Save the Children cannot guarantee this assistance.

* Save the Children Safety and Security Policy and
Standards – Standard 11, February 2010

 **Save the Children**

management being forced to leave. However, this must only be done with staff consent and involvement. Staff must never be pressurised to continue their work if this would expose them to any danger.

Each plan should be developed for a specific context, but should always include details on: the decision-making process; what would trigger the withdrawal of staff; security levels and associated procedures; evacuation routes; communication procedures; administrative procedures; essential emergency supplies; and checklists. All plans must be reviewed and updated regularly.

10 RELOCATING AND EVACUATING STAFF

Decision-making process

It is important that all staff clearly understand the circumstances in which a relocation or evacuation from a particular site would be considered and the decision-making process. The plan should clearly define:

- Relationship between the withdrawal of staff and the security levels and indicators for that location.

When to withdraw

Within Save the Children, the authority to order the relocation of staff (in-country), to suspend operations, or temporarily close an office for security reasons, lies with the Country Director. The authority to order the evacuation of international staff lies with Regional/Area Director in close consultation with the Director of Global Programmes.[*]

In cases where a threat is imminent, the Country Director may take the decision to evacuate international staff without prior consultation. If such a decision is taken, the Country Director must notify the Regional/Area Director and Director of Global Programmes at the earliest possible time.

Refusal of a Save the Children staff member to evacuate or relocate may result in that staff member's dismissal. Regardless of the reason, any Save the Children staff member and their dependants refusing an evacuation/relocation order must acknowledge in writing that they remain at their own risk and that Save the Children will not accept responsibility for their safety.

[*] Save the Children Safety and Security Policy and Standards – Standard 11, February 2010

- Who takes the decision to suspend activities, or relocate or evacuate staff.
- Who co-ordinates the process.
- How the decision is taken in the event of absence or loss of communication or a sudden emergency.

Any staff member has the right to leave if they feel the security risks are unacceptable. No one should ever be forced to stay in a location against their will, and they should be relocated or evacuated, as long as their withdrawal has no impact on the security of others.

Relocation/evacuation procedures

Relocation/evacuation plans should outline the procedures and various tasks associated with the withdrawal of staff, including:

- Roles and responsibilities of staff members at each security level.
- Methods for notifying staff of a suspension in activities or their imminent withdrawal.
- How to prepare for imminent withdrawal, with details on who is responsible for each task.
- How and what to communicate to local officials, partner organisations and colleagues.
- Instructions on how to move from one site to another and where to assemble for a relocation or evacuation.
- What items to bring and what to leave behind (eg, money, passport, food, first-aid kit) and the amount of personal luggage permitted (often 15kg).
- Contingency plans for communications, safe havens and routes if original plans fail.

Routes and transportation

Information on travel methods and routes must be as specific as possible and cover all options; for example, using commercial or military air transport. Maps demarcating pick-up points, potential landing sites for aircraft, and estimated travel times should also be included. Alternative routes and methods of travel must be considered and prioritised if the original options turn out to be no longer safe or feasible.

In the event that evacuation to a neighbouring country is required, plans should also give guidance about border-crossing, indicating when it should occur, where it is safe to cross, the procedures for crossing, and how to make contact with the appropriate authorities in the neighbouring country.

In the event that it is not possible to relocate or evacuate, the plan should indicate hibernation points (safe areas) for each location, how to reach them, and contact persons there. Safe areas may include a bunker/secure room in your agency's compound, UN offices, government structures or national staff houses.

Communication

Effective communication is the key to crisis management. Emergency communication procedures – who is to contact staff and key groups such as other agencies, and how – must be put in place in advance and be stipulated in the relocation/evacuation plan. Developing these networks prior to an emergency reduces the chance of a breakdown in communication or misunderstanding at the moment of crisis. It is important to ensure that all emergency communication is short, clear and factual. During a relocation/evacuation a schedule for regular radio or telephone contact must be established and maintained continuously.

Administrative procedures

The relocation/evacuation plan should specify what administrative and financial procedures must be followed in the event of the withdrawal of staff, and what preparation should take place beforehand. Issues may include: paying local staff salaries; ensuring that staff have appropriate travel/exit documents; clarifying what funds should be left with remaining staff to cover running costs; and what important documentation should be removed and by whom.

Equipment and supplies

Plans should include details of emergency supplies required for each location (ie, drinking water, food stocks, medical supplies and fuel reserves) and where these should be kept. In the event of hibernation, staff may be confined in the same building for hours, days or even weeks. It's important to ensure that adequate supplies and facilities are available. Plans should also clearly indicate which assets, if any, should be withdrawn, by whom and when. In all cases, the safety of personnel must always take priority over personal property or agency assets.

Checklists

The relocation/evacuation plan should incorporate accessible, easy-to-read checklists and other resources, which can be invaluable reminders or sources of information to staff. Helpful checklists should include:

- Staff details: list of passport numbers; expiry dates; location of passport for each staff member; names of staff members with special medical needs; blood groups.
- Complete information on assembly points: who should go where and when; means of transportation; maps, including those showing staff housing, embassies, other agency bases, key facilities and travel routes.
- Contact information and communication networks: list of other agencies, local government offices, and individuals who could be a resource during an emergency (including names, addresses, telephone numbers, radio locations and frequencies). These should be carried by staff at all times.
- List of food, water and emergency supplies to be kept in staff residences, assembly sites and safe havens.
- List of essential items to include in an emergency grab bag.

WHEN TO RETURN

Once the crisis has passed or the security situation has stabilised, the area should be reassessed to determine whether it is safe enough to return. The decision to return should be made in consultation with all staff, giving them ample opportunity to discuss their concerns and the possible consequences of returning.

Authorisation to return

When Save the Children international staff have been evacuated, authorisation to return to the country can only be given by the Director of Global Programmes.[*] The decision as to when to return will be determined in consultation with the Regional or Area Director and the Country Director, once a security assessment has been undertaken.

[*] Save the Children Safety and Security Policy and Standards – Standard 11, February 2010

---

11 INCIDENT MONITORING

It is essential that you are aware of, and that you understand, any safety and security incidents that happen in your working environment, in order to ensure the overall protection of staff. A well-maintained system for timely reporting and analysis of incidents that affect you, your colleagues or others in the area, can help you identify, analyse and react to changes in the security situation.

Incidents occurring in the field should be routinely reported to your agency's regional and head offices. This will improve the organisation-wide understanding of the environments in which your agency operates and will enable the organisation to monitor and react to any developing trends affecting the safety and security of personnel.

WHAT IS AN INCIDENT?

Perceptions as to what constitutes a security or safety incident will vary significantly between individuals and locations. One person may feel that a short exchange of gunfire during the night is not worth reporting, while another may consider it a disturbing event. Harassment of staff at a checkpoint might be almost a daily occurrence in one location, but in another it could indicate a serious deterioration in security. In an environment where incidents occur on a daily basis, it may seem impractical to report each one. Yet it's vital not to miss seemingly isolated and insignificant incidences that, when viewed together, may signify a change in the security situation. If in doubt, report it.

Timely reporting and analysis of incidents can help you identify and react to changes in the security situation.

A security or safety incident is any event that seriously affects the physical or emotional wellbeing of staff or results in substantial damage, or loss, to the organisation's property or programme activities. It is also any significant event that affects another humanitarian agency, or individuals or groups within the wider population, indicating a change in the security situation. As a team you must carefully consider what are significant incidents for your location and context, and make sure all staff have clear guidance on which types of safety and security incidents need to be reported.

Equally important is the reporting of any 'near miss' incident where, either through luck or appropriate procedures, a serious incident was narrowly avoided. You must also report any threats or warnings, or 'advice' issued to yourself, your colleagues or to the wider humanitarian community that constitutes a significant security threat.

Incidents are often preceded by some sort of suspicious activity; for example, staff may be followed or your office watched. Reporting any such suspicions or concerns could help avoid a potentially more serious incident.

INCIDENT REPORTING AND PROCEDURES

The process of reporting security incidents should in itself be simple and not time-consuming. However, it's important that agencies have standardised incident reporting procedures that ensure consistency and clearly outline to staff the types of incidents that should be reported, to whom and in what format.

Types of incident reports

There are typically four types of incident reports:
- **Immediate incident report**. This is normally verbal and sent as soon as possible after the start of the incident, often by radio or phone, and contains only a brief summary of what has happened.
- **Incident updates**. These are sent as often as necessary while the incident or response to the incident continues. An incident update can be used to provide any information on changes to the situation, or to provide additional details that it was not possible to give during the immediate incident report.
- **Formal incident report**. This is usually written and sent once the incident has been stabilised or resolved.
- **Incident log and mapping**. This is a record or map of all incidents, or near misses, that have been reported over a given period, so that incidents can be easily analysed in relation to other incidents.

Reporting an incident

If you are involved in or observe a security incident, you should report it to your manager/base as soon as it is safe to do so. Initial information is often sketchy and things may be confusing, so take your time to assess what has happened, how safe you are, and what assistance you need. Information should be provided in a clear, concise manner and should include:

- **Who** the incident happened to
- **What** happened
- **Where** the incident occurred
- **When** the incident occurred
- **What** you have done about it
- **What** help you need.

If there is no time, or it is unsafe, to provide all of the above while the incident is ongoing, provide whatever is possible. For example, even just reporting 'we are being ambushed!' will at least alert colleagues to what is happening, so that they can work out how to respond, and how to avoid the same danger. Even the briefest of information could save lives.

Formal incident reports

A formal incident report, providing a complete written account of the incident and the various actions that were taken, should be produced as

---

Reporting incidents

Save the Children requires that all safety and security incidents, including 'near misses', be reported immediately to the Country Director, who in turn is required to report all incidents upwards, within 24 hours. Critical incidents must be reported immediately, by telephone, to the Regional Director and respective Senior Specialist for Regional Safety and Security (SSRSS).[*]

All safety and security incident reports must be submitted using SC Reporter – Save the Children's web-based incident reporting system. Reports are then automatically copied to the appropriate designated regional, area and head office personnel.

[*] Save the Children Safety and Security Policy and Standards – Standard 10, February 2010

 Save the Children

soon as possible after the incident, in a calm and safe environment. This report should include:

- **Type of incident**. It's important to be clear as to the type of incident; for example, robbery, armed robbery, theft, vehicle accident, etc.
- **Location**. Describe where the incident occurred as precisely as possible.
- **Date, day and time**. Describe when the incident occurred as precisely as possible.
- **Description of the incident**. Describe the nature of the incident and the events, including who was involved, who perpetrated/what caused the incident, the impact on those affected, and details of any material losses, etc.
- **Decisions and actions taken**. Detail any decisions and actions taken, and by whom, immediately after the incident.
- **Who has been informed**. Detail who the incident has been reported to locally – eg, authorities, agencies and other actors, etc.
- **Implications for staff and programmes**. Highlight the possible implications of the incident for the safety and security of staff.
- **Any further actions to be taken**. Detail the decisions and actions that you will be taking in response to the incident. State any recommendations for improving the safety and security of staff.

Incident log and mapping

In addition to the formal incident reports, agencies should also maintain a centralised record of the different safety and security incidents that occur in a particular location. The incident log should summarise and map the key information associated with safety and security incidents that affect staff or property. This incident overview is extremely important, as it will enable you and your successors to monitor and analyse patterns and trends in incidents, and therefore draw out further analysis. These records also provide an easily accessible institutional record of the various incidents that have occurred in that location.

INCIDENT ANALYSIS

After an incident has been reported, you need to consider why it occurred despite the safety and security procedures and guidelines already in place, and what actions should be taken to minimise the chances of it happening again. An incident analysis should investigate the following key areas in depth:*

- **Motives and behaviour**. What are the possible motives of the perpetrators of the incident? Were the underlying motives financial, social, cultural or political? What may have triggered the actions of the perpetrators? Did your agency or any staff member have a role in provoking the incident through a particular act or statement or by their behaviour?

LAURENT DUVILLIER/SAVE THE CHILDREN

Incident analysis may expose gaps in your safety and security measures, and help you better understand the environment in which you are operating.

- **Targeting**. Are there any indications that the incident was opportunistic, or were you targeted? If the latter, were you a target because you are an international organisation, or was your agency specifically targeted?
- **Patterns**. Are there emerging patterns/trends in the locations, timings, targets or victims of incidents that have implications for security? (The quality of your pattern analysis will depend on the reliability and detail of previous incident reports and analysis.)
- **Effectiveness of procedures**. Were safety and security measures in place to tackle the incident? How effective were these procedures? Were they clearly communicated to, understood and followed by all staff? What could have been managed better?

Whether or not the incident has affected your agency, serious security incidents should immediately lead to a review of the security situation and the measures you currently have in place. This incident analysis may expose gaps in your safety and security measures, and can help you and your staff to better understand the environment in which you are operating.

12 INFORMATION MANAGEMENT

Good security management rests on a number of straightforward principles. One of these principles is the fundamental obligation on the part of all agencies to ensure that mechanisms and procedures are in place that facilitate the flow of security-related information. Security information and details of incidents must be shared internally with all staff, and externally with other agencies operating in the same environment. This ensures that everyone is fully aware of developments in the security situation and that they can react appropriately. Another important principle is that all staff must be mindful of the way in which they handle information in the field, as this can have a direct effect on their own personal security, and that of their colleagues, other agencies and beneficiaries.

The relationship between NGOs and the media is another important element in the management of information and can be vital for the security of staff. The media can play a critical role in alerting governments and the wider public to security issues and problems of safe access. In some contexts, well-managed media coverage has triggered actions by authorities and other key parties to improve security for humanitarian agencies, where other channels of communication and lobbying have failed. Equally, carefully considered media work can help reduce or remove certain security threats by gaining widespread acceptance for an agency's presence and work in a country. On the other hand, ill-prepared or impulsive statements or negative coverage in the media can undermine the image and acceptance of an agency, which ultimately may endanger the lives of staff and beneficiaries.

SHARING INFORMATION

It is crucial to disseminate safety and security information to all staff, and regularly discuss the risks as a team. This enables staff to develop a more detailed understanding of the situation and can ensure better responses to safety and security incidents when they occur. While security discussions often take place during regular programme meetings, it's important to also establish specific mechanisms that can help improve the dissemination of security information to all staff – for example:

- Organising specific staff security meetings on a regular basis so that all staff have an adequate opportunity to raise and discuss their safety and security concerns and how the agency is dealing with them.

Security information must be shared with all staff and other agencies to ensure that everyone is fully aware of developments in the security situation and can react appropriately.

- Placing security reports and advisory notices on staff notice boards, or in a central area in the office, to ensure that all staff are kept informed. Remember that not all staff members will have access to email.
- Establishing an internal SMS text-based 'communication tree' to ensure that staff are instantly informed of security incidents or potential dangers. In most countries, staff have access to mobile phones. Free software that enables bulk SMS messaging is now widely available.
- Organising half-day or lunch-time discussions or trainings on specific safety and security issues; for example, carjacking, dealing with personal threats, or basic first aid.

Just as staff must be made aware of security incidents and changes in the security situation, so must other agencies. No agency operates in a vacuum, and what affects the security of one agency will almost certainly affect the security of others. Each agency will interpret and react differently to a particular incident or security situation; each has its own threshold for what it considers to be an acceptable level of risk. Therefore, it's important that you actively share security information with other agencies to allow them to make their own judgements on changing security situations and how to deal with them.

Over recent years greater emphasis has been placed on inter-agency security collaboration. Agencies have formed various collaborative networks, forums and mechanisms to facilitate the exchange of security information in the field; for example, regular inter-agency security meetings

---

Communication trees

All Save the Children Country Offices must establish a staff 'communication tree' so as to contact all staff when necessary. This communication tree must be regularly updated.*

* Save the Children Safety and Security Policy and
Standards – Standard 9, February 2010

and briefings, establishing SMS text-based 'security trees' or warden systems to rapidly transmit security incident reports and alerts to agencies, and in some contexts setting up a dedicated safety and security office to provide support and information to the entire NGO community.

INFORMATION SECURITY AND PRIVACY

While all agencies should strive for openness and transparency, there will be situations when this must be balanced with the need to be discreet with certain information. Information regarding security incidents and political or military developments can be perceived in certain contexts as sensitive, or may contradict the 'official' version of events. In some countries, interference and monitoring by the authorities of agency communications is a serious problem, and organisations and individual aid workers have been deported, arrested or threatened because of the information they've collated, or the information they've communicated internally or externally. Information about staff, financial procedures or programme activities and plans could, in the wrong hands, expose the organisation and staff to increased threats from criminal activity.

It's important to develop security-conscious habits as you go about your daily work when collating, storing, communicating and disposing of sensitive information, especially if the information could expose staff or beneficiaries to greater risk.

Securing information

All Save the Children Country Offices must ensure that sensitive and confidential information is appropriately secured, and must establish clear guidance for the protection of sensitive/confidential information.*

* Save the Children Safety and Security Policy and Standards – Standard 9, February 2010

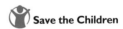 Save the Children

---

It's important to develop security-conscious habits when collating, storing, communicating and disposing of sensitive information.

Information security

Information security is not about being covert or secretive; it is essentially about developing 'good housekeeping' to ensure that all information is managed safely and securely, and that there is adequate protection from theft, loss or unauthorised access. Secure management of information involves both physical and procedural measures.

Ensure the physical security of information in the office:
- Keep the office locked at all times, including doors and windows.
- Keep a track of keys to the office and who has access to these.
- Make sure someone is always present when visitors, maintenance staff or cleaning staff are in the office.

- Lock computers away, if possible, when leaving the office, or use cable locks to secure them to your desk.
- Don't leave sensitive documents lying on your desk.
- If possible, make sure you have a secure room or locked filing cabinets where files can be kept. Sensitive documents should be stored in the office safe.

Be mindful of information you collate, how it's stored and who has access to it:

- Ensure that sensitive information, files and data cannot be accessed without appropriate authorisation. Not all staff should have access to all information.
- Make sure that your computer has a good password (minimum eight characters long and including numbers and/or special characters) and change this regularly. Do not write down User IDs or passwords.
- Consider using encryption software to protect key files or documents in case someone accesses your computer and removes the hard drive.
- Consider unplugging or disabling your computer's Internet connection when leaving the machine unattended.
- Make sure you regularly back up your data and keep it in a secure, separate location.
- Keep personnel files, staff travel movements and contact details confidential and share only with the responsible staff. Do not give out colleagues' addresses or telephone numbers.
- When travelling, be mindful of the information that's stored on your laptop and make sure that there's nothing that could compromise you or your organisation if it were stolen, or inspected at customs.
- If you think that the information on your computer may have been accessed without your authorisation, report this to your manager.

Safe communications

Significant advances in technology mean that it's now even easier to communicate while working in remote locations. However, these same advances also mean that it's now easier for others to monitor your communications. Most voice communication – radio, landline, mobile phone, and even satellite communication – can be monitored by someone who wishes to do so and has enough technological capacity. No phone call, particularly via a mobile phone, can be assumed to be secure, because both your location and your conversations can easily be picked up through cellular surveillance.

Email scanning is widespread in some countries. Your email does not go directly from your computer to the intended recipient's computer. It goes through several routes and can be intercepted and scanned for key words at various points in the message's routing.

When communicating information, make sure you adopt safe communication practices:
- Always assume that your conversations or emails could be monitored, and therefore be conscious of what you say or write.
- Password-protecting emails and attachments does very little to protect the information. If you want to send a file or email more securely you must use encryption. Be aware that the use of encryption is not permitted in certain countries, and in others it can draw unwanted attention from the authorities, who will be suspicious of the information you are sending.
- If you need to communicate sensitive information, the use of peer-to-peer-based applications such as Skype can offer better security, as they use encryption to protect all voice calls, chat messages and file transfers.
- Be careful when sending group emails. You could unknowingly implicate others by the content of the email, or the following replies, or associate them with other recipients.
- Remember that no message is 100% secure, so think before sending it!

Blogging and social media

In recent years there has been an explosion in the use of social media by aid workers. Social media is an umbrella term that encompasses various online tools such as blogs, twitter, social networking sites, wikis, forums, and photo- and video-sharing sites. Many aid workers actively participate in social media by contributing to online discussion forums or by establishing their own personal blogs to share their experiences in the field. Although these emerging social media tools offer huge benefits to the aid sector, their use by aid workers in some politically sensitive contexts has led to additional security risks, and a number of aid workers have been harassed, threatened, detained or deported as a result of content or comments they have posted online.

When creating a personal blog or participating in online social networks, discussion forums or any other form of social media, you should follow these basic guidelines:

- Always remember that what you post will be freely available and open to being republished in other media.
- Make sure your comments are respectful to others, and do not make remarks that could be considered insensitive or offensive.
- Do not disclose confidential or sensitive information that may place other colleagues, other agencies or beneficiaries at risk.
- Always respect the fundamental principles of your organisation and abide by the staff code of conduct.
- If your personal blog or profile identifies you as working for a particular agency, always make clear that the views you're expressing are yours alone and not necessarily those of your agency. Even so, think carefully about whether the personal thoughts or comments you publish might still be misunderstood as expressing your agency's position.
- Even if you are blogging anonymously, be aware that it may be easy for people to work out who you are, where you are working and the agency you're working for, from the comments you make or the pictures you post.
- Be careful about joining, or indicating your support for, campaigning groups on social network sites that the authorities may view as antagonistic.
- If you're thinking about posting something on your blog or in a discussion group that may give rise to concerns, discuss it with your line manager before posting.

Disposal of information

In addition to managing the information in your office and how it is communicated, you should also pay careful attention to how you dispose of this information when it's no longer needed. There have been incidents where confidential and sensitive information has been discovered in waste bins outside an agency's office. Follow these basic guidelines:

- All waste paper and documents should be shredded and then, if possible, burnt before disposal.
- When disposing of old computers, CDs or data storage devices, make sure you erase everything using a file-shredding program. Merely deleting files from the computer is not enough, as some information will always remain and could be retrieved.

WORKING WITH THE MEDIA

In general, journalists should be viewed as an opportunity rather than a threat: with careful planning and targeting, you will find them useful allies in getting your message across. But journalists have a job to do, uncovering 'news', and therefore it's important that this relationship is carefully managed.

In some situations, because of concerns regarding security or sensitivity, an agency may prefer to keep a low profile and limit contact with the media or avoid discussing certain subjects. Normally your agency's media office or your line manager will advise you on handling the media coverage of situations in which you are working. These decisions must be respected.

What to say to the media

Contact between your organisation and the media should ideally be channelled through senior management or the media office. In practice, however, this is not always possible. Field staff often find themselves approached without any advance notice by journalists already on the ground. In such circumstances, the key is to appear positive and helpful, and observe the following basic guidelines:

- If you are approached for an on-the-spot interview by a journalist and are unable to oblige because of pressure of work, refuse politely.
- If you feel a photographer or camera operative is being intrusive, do not lose your cool. Explain the problem and the constraints you're working under. Politely ask them to leave and arrange an appointment for a more appropriate time.
- If you are asked to make a comment, provide some general information on your agency and its activities, but don't get drawn into commenting on the political or military situation.
- Do not complain, however light-heartedly, about the host government, local authorities, or other national or international organisations. Such remarks can very easily be distorted. Constructive criticism is sometimes necessary, but this should be left to senior management and to the press office.

Engaging with the media

Save the Children's Country Directors should wherever possible consult the Media Unit at Head Office before engaging with the media. If the issue is controversial, or if there are any problems, they should consult the Regional or Area Director and/or Head of Media.

Wherever possible, staff must seek clearance from the Country Director, or Media Manager, before agreeing to be interviewed by journalists. In some cases, the Country Director may assign certain members of staff to be spokespersons.

Country Directors should alert the Media Unit at Head Office if they know something is about to appear in the media as a result of staff speaking to journalists.

Further information can be found in Save the Children's *Emergency Communications Toolkit*, 2009.

 Save the Children

Always think carefully about possible security implications. In some situations, association with journalists or media might compromise the safety of staff.

- Do not be tempted to give 'off the record' comments. If you give a journalist a good story, you can hardly blame them for using it. Anyone speaking to the media as an official representative should remember that what they say reflects on the organisation as a whole, and not just on one particular project.
- If a journalist requests more information, or if you're worried about what to say, refer them to your line manager or your agency's media office.

Handling interviews

As well as gathering information from aid agencies, the media often like to interview staff directly in the field. Interviews can be difficult, and therefore they should normally be handled by staff experienced at being interviewed. However, your agency may request you to undertake the interview. If so, you should observe the following basic interview techniques:

- If you're not aware of the programme or publication the journalist represents, ask about its audience. This may influence what and how much information you give.
- Be clear about what they want to talk about. Ask them to run through the topics they want to cover before you start. Don't be afraid to state the limitations on what you're prepared to talk about.
- Be clear in your own mind about the message you want to convey. Before the interview, take some time to gather your thoughts, then narrow them down to three or four main points.
- Stick to the facts. If you don't know the answer, just say so. Don't be drawn into speculation about what might happen or what you think may occur next, as this can be easily misinterpreted.
- Don't let the interviewer put words into your mouth. If you disagree with something, say so.
- Keep it simple and don't use jargon and acronyms. Remember that you may be addressing a wide and varied audience.

Relationships with journalists

Before agreeing to help journalists in the field – for example, by providing them with transport or accommodation – always think carefully about the possible security implications. In places where association with certain journalists or media might compromise your organisation's work and jeopardise the safety of staff, exercise particular caution. Journalists should never be permitted to identify themselves as being part of your agency's team. Always consult your line manager or your agency's media office before agreeing to any request for assistance.

BIBLIOGRAPHY

Bessler, M and McHugh, G (2006) *Humanitarian Negotiations with Armed Groups: A Manual for Practitioners*, New York, UN Office for the Coordination of Humanitarian Affairs (OCHA)

Briggs, R (2001) *The Kidnapping Business*, London, The Foreign Policy Centre

Cutts, M and Dingle, A (1998) *Safety First: Protecting NGO employees who work in areas of conflict*, London, Save the Children

Davidson, S and Neal, I (1998) *Under Cover? Insurance for aid workers*, London, People in Aid

Davis, J (1998) *Landmines: Security Training Module for NGOs*, Office of US Foreign Disaster Assistance (OFDA)/InterAction

Davis, J (1998) *Site Security: Security Training Module for NGOs*, Office of US Foreign Disaster Assistance (OFDA)/InterAction

Davis, J (1998) *Vehicles and Vehicle Travel: Security Training Module for NGOs*, Office of US Foreign Disaster Assistance (OFDA)/InterAction

Davis, J and Lambert, R (2002) *Engineering In Emergencies: A Practical Guide For Relief Workers*, London, Intermediate Technology Publications

Deen, T (2006) *International Aid Work: A Deadly Profession*, Inter Press Service

Dworken, J T (1998) *Threat Assessment: Training Module for NGOs Operating in Conflict Zones and High Crime Areas*, Office of US Foreign Disaster Assistance (OFDA)/InterAction

Lankester, T (2002) *The Travellers' Good Health Guide*, London, Sheldon Press

Lowe, R (1998) *Telecommunications: Security Training Module for NGOs*, Office of US Foreign Disaster Assistance (OFDA)/InterAction

McGrath, R (1994) *Landmines: Legacy of Conflict, A Manual for Development Workers*, Oxford, Oxfam

O'Neil, M (1998) *Evacuation Plan*, Office of US Foreign Disaster Assistance (OFDA)/InterAction

Roberts, D L (1999) *Staying Alive: Safety and Security Guidelines for Humanitarian Volunteers in Conflict Areas*, Geneva, International Committee of the Red Cross

Rodgers, C and Sytsma, B (1999) *World Vision Security Manual: Safety Awareness for Aid Workers*, Geneva, World Vision

Sheik, M (2000) 'Deaths among humanitarian workers', *British Medical Journal*, 321: 166–168

Stoddard, A, Harmer, A and Haver, K (2006) *Providing Aid in Insecure Environments: Trends in Policy and Operations*, London, Overseas Development Institute

Stoddard, A, Harmer, A and Di Domenico, V (2009) *Providing Aid in Insecure Environments: 2009 Update*, London, Overseas Development Institute

Van Brabant, K (2000) *Operational Security Management in Violent Environments*, Good Practice Review 8, London, Overseas Development Institute

Van Brabant, K (2001) *Mainstreaming the Organisational Management of Safety and Security: A review of aid agency principles and a guide for management*, London, Overseas Development Institute

Be Safe Be Secure: Security Guidelines for Women (2006) New York, United Nations Department of Safety and Security

Civil–military Guidelines & Reference For Complex Emergencies (2008) New York, Inter-Agency Standing Committee/UN Office for the Coordination of Humanitarian Affairs (OCHA)

Generic Security Guide for Humanitarian Organisations (2004) Brussels, European Commission's DG-ECHO

Humanitarian Action and Armed Conflict: Coping with stress (2001) Geneva, International Committee of the Red Cross

NGO Security Collaboration Guide (2006) Brussels, European Commission's DG-ECHO

Security Awareness: An Aide-mémoire (1995) Geneva, Office of the United Nations High Commissioner for Refugees

Security in the Field: Information for staff members of the United Nations system (1998) New York, United Nations

Security of Relief Workers and Humanitarian Space – ECHO Working Paper (1998) Brussels, European Commission

Security Risk Management: NGO Approach (2009) InterAction,

Stay Safe: The International Federation's guide for security managers (2007) Geneva, International Federation of Red Cross and Red Crescent Societies

Stay Safe: The International Federation's guide to a safer mission (2007) Geneva, International Federation of Red Cross and Red Crescent Societies